GOVERNMENTS AND MONEY

GOVERNMENTS AND MONEY

With special reference to financial legislation in the United States, and the establishment of an International Standard of Trade

BY

EDWARD JEROME

BOSTON

LITTLE, BROWN, AND COMPANY

1935

CONTENTS

GOVERNMENTS AND MONEY

CHAPTER I

HOW MONEY WAS EVOLVED

EVERYONE recognizes money as the immediate means of acquiring goods and the services of other men; but its direct and effective use tends to mislead inquirers into its real nature. Money is not a thing in itself, capable of performing its functions alone, but is an instrument used in the distribution of goods, which is neither begun by money nor entirely dependent upon it. In the beginning attention should be concentrated upon that distributive process as a whole.

In comparatively few societies has there been any conscious organization of facilities for the distribution of goods. The natural desire of men to satisfy their wants has been relied upon as the impulse which causes exchanges; but an exchange is either the handing over of one thing for another thing, or the rendering of a service for either a thing or another service. Money is not required for the making of such exchanges, as they were made with the greatest ease and facility long before money was ever conceived; and it is probable that its creation has done more to retard the making of exchanges than to help. The commercial practices of men have always caused the adoption of some satisfactory medium of exchange even without the creation of money by governments. A medium of exchange may exist without its being money.

There is a distinction between the exchange of goods and the distribution of goods. It seems a more accurate view to regard rewards for services as entitling those who render service to share in the distribution of goods, rather than as an exchange of services for goods. That is suggested by Adam Smith's references to money as the "Great Wheel of Circulation", and as the "great but expensive instrument of commerce, by means of which every individual in the society has his subsistence, conveniences, and amusements regularly distributed to him in their proper proportions." [1]

In other words, it seems better to regard money as a means of measuring and distributing the share of each citizen in the goods available for distribu-

[1] "Wealth of Nations", Book II, Ch. 2.

4

tion, rather than as a "measure of value", which is the commonly accepted view.

A detailed inquiry into the nature of the functions of money must be preceded by naming the instruments which accompany its use, and by considering the functions of the instrument which begins the process of distributing goods.

There are, and have been used, three methods of distributing to members of a society the goods available for their consumption. The first and most primitive method is an equal distribution based solely upon *membership* in the particular society, without the use of any intermediary instrument. Usually such a distribution is greatly affected by the fact that the share of each member cannot be more than what is required by bare necessity. In societies of this kind money has rarely, if ever, been used, although it may be.

When used in such a society, the instrument by which money is preceded is the intangible one of relations involved in membership in the society. To this stage there need be given little consideration, except to observe that a primitive society of this kind probably would engage collectively in barter either with another tribe or with its individual members. That, however, would not involve the use of money, and the sole instrument of distribution would remain membership in the society.

The second method of distribution is to be found in a society in which the share of individual members in its available "subsistence, conveniences, and amusements" is determined according to their *status* in the society. The headsman, lord, or prince acquires goods and distributes to his dependents little more than is absolutely necessary. This distribution is not through exchanges, but to each man according to his condition. Such a society probably has some goods in excess of those needed for the bare existence of its members, and thus the foundation is laid for the private possession and use of things. This introduces complications in the process of distribution, and something which is in the nature of money, answers its purpose, or is a substitute for it usually appears soon after such a stage is reached. Its development into money will be considered later; here emphasis must be given to the fact that the instrument which precedes the use of a substitute for money in a society of this kind is still primarily the relation of membership, with such complications

6

as are introduced by the subjection of that relation to the additional one of status.

The use of money by a society of this kind is under conditions which are entirely different from those which prevail in the distribution of goods by a society that follows the third method — which is generally prevalent to-day, and to which some preliminary attention must now be given.

It was observed by Sir Henry Maine that the trend of all progressive societies has been to make relations between men depend upon *contract* instead of status.[2] There is no concern here with whether

[2] Maine's "Ancient Law", p. 165. In Lipson's "Economic History of England", p. 87 (A. & C. Black. Ltd., London, 1915), the occurrence of this trend in England is commented upon: —

But while these facts must be taken into consideration, the remarkable increase of free labour within thirty years after the pestilence indicates how enormous was the influence which it exercised upon the economic situation. The Black Death constituted a landmark in the historical evolution of the English peasantry from servitude to freedom. It gave a violent shock to the ancient manorial arrangements and weakened irreparably the stability of the rural framework of mediaeval society.

However difficult it may be to measure the exact significance of the Black Death, it is certain that the hundred years which followed witnessed the complete disintegration of the old manorial order. The influences which had hitherto militated against the disappearance of villeinage, and had worked to preserve intact the system of unfree tenures, ceased to operate. The labour conditions of the country were transformed by the permeation of social forces, which called into existence a new agrarian organization and established a new set of

that trend was a cause or a result of progress, or indeed with whether it accompanied progress or retrogression, but with the fact that there was such a trend. From the very beginning of the recognition by the social group of individual possession and exclusive use of land and things, there arose those relations between men with respect to things which are to-day denoted by the term "contract."

The definitions of a contract ordinarily to be found — one of which is "a promise, or a set of promises, to which the law attaches legal obligation" [8] — must not, for present purposes, be given a meaning with too narrow limits of extension. There can-

---

economic relations. The drift of the movement was in fact nothing less than the substitution of a society, organized on the basis of free contractual relations, for a society based upon tenure and status; a society in which the customary relations between lord and tenant were superseded by a uniform legal bond and cash nexus. The plague, which lasted for fourteen months, from August 1348 to the autumn of 1349, is believed to have swept away one-half of the entire population. The figures of the chroniclers are to be accepted with caution, but the diocesan institution books and the court rolls of manors afford irrefragable testimony that the mortality was overwhelming, and the effects were bound therefore to be far-reaching. To begin with, it is natural to suppose that the money per head of the population was as good as doubled, if the population were halved while the currency remained unaffected. This would facilitate the growth of commutation by affording the villeins the means of turning their services into money payments.

[8] Williston on Contracts, p. 1, Sec. 1.

8

not be an exchange of one thing for another, of work for a thing, a promise for a promise, or of one kind of work for another kind, without a resulting contract. Even when the promise is so hidden as to seem nonexistent, nevertheless it may be there by customary implication, and its obligation may be just as binding as if expressed in an engraved bond, signed and sealed.

In this third method of distributing goods, the contract finally became the great, all-important instrument through which a member of society acquired the money which served as the immediate means of obtaining his share of the "subsistence, conveniences, and amusements" available for distribution in the society. This stage of development, however, was a long time in coming; and it came so gradually that men failed to notice the great difference between the functions which money was called upon to perform in a society where every man had to have some kind of contract in order to exist, or else be an object of charity, and the functions of a commodity medium of exchange in a society in which few men could make contracts, but most of them were dependent upon their status for a living.

This is a most important point, and one that has

been given little attention. Money was developed by that stage of society in which distribution of goods to individual members was largely determined by their status; that method of distribution passed away or was abandoned, but the ideas about money now prevalent are largely a survival or inheritance from this period, without due allowance for the great changes in commerce and industry, government, and law that have since occurred.

"The economic development of a nation shows itself . . . in an organization of credit. Primitive barter allowed of none; it proceeded on a system of give and take." [4] *Money* thus finally came to serve as a kind of common denominator in which the terms of a contract could be expressed. The use of money in any kind of business transaction is always preceded by a contract, and the development of the two instruments must be considered together. As that requires a brief glance backward in time, it seems best to give here a summary statement of the nature of the modern process, the development of which is the subject of consideration.

Contracts have been mentioned as the first important instrument with which all modern societies

[4] J. Declareuil, "Rome the Law-giver", p. 258.

begin the distribution of goods. Then the process is carried further with money; and after that facilitated by another instrument, which is generally described as a bank. Thus the third method of distributing goods, which begins with *contracts,* is carried on with *money,* and is then facilitated by banks, may be called the *monetary process.* Now the process itself has gone on from the time of the first business transaction, the first exchange of goods; but the customary methods according to which it has been conducted have caused the appearance of different institutions to play their parts in the process. A definition has been given the first instrument, and one may be given the third at this point, but the definition of the second, or money, depends upon its functions, which have not been considered adequately enough for the purpose. A bank, however, may be defined as an institution the business of which consists of making and performing contracts to pay money. With the observation that the business of banking is not to be confused with the creation of money, — as frequently it is confused, — further consideration of the modern monetary process must be postponed for an examination of the principles upon which it has evolved.

Always it is the nature of the transaction in the affairs of men which must be kept in mind. The attention is not to be concentrated upon things, but upon motives, ideas, and methods. An origin of all business transactions is to be found in the exchange of articles from the hands of one party to those of the other when each simultaneously grasps the thing the other is giving up. There is then no confidence, which prevents the exchange of an article by one party for a promise of the other person to deliver a different kind of article in the future. As soon as that confidence grows to be great enough for the parties to trust each other by exchanging things for promises, either to do some kind of work or to deliver another thing, custom begins to play its part. This separation of the two acts in time, as well as in space, depends upon confidence and custom, the entrance of which, even in the most primitive societies, gradually proceeds to develop a law of contracts. Customary methods of dealing with those who made contracts and did not perform them became stamped upon the memories of men, then committed to writing, and finally to be recognized as statements of the law of contracts. The conception of a contract is the result of immemorial custom rather than of positive enactments or declarations. That contracts may be made is a fundamental assumption arising by necessary implication from the very existence of exclusive private possession of land and things. The system called Capitalism would be much more appropriately described as a Contractual System, as it depends for its success upon general observance of two great principles. As has been previously observed, the entrance of contracts had to wait for the growth of confidence, which shows that the first of these two universal laws is that contracts shall be inviolable. Chief Justice Marshall said that one great purpose of the Constitutional Convention held in the United States in 1787 was to make contracts inviolable.[5] The second of these fundamental laws of the system is that there shall be freedom of contract. Any general observance of this law is a long time coming in any society; and the gradual movement toward it is to be considered here, more than the development of the law of contracts.

In tracing the broad outlines of the movement toward freedom of contract, it must be kept in mind that there were two classes of restrictions to be re-

[5] Sturges *v.* Crowinshield, 4 Wheaton, 122, at 206.

moved. The first was upon the number of men who were free to make contracts, and the second upon the kind of contracts which could be made and the manner in which they might be performed. In ancient times, or perhaps it should be said in more primitive societies, restrictions of the first class had the more important results and were more prevalent, while in advanced societies the latter class of restrictions are more numerous and important.

The great change in the method of distributing goods was not caused by the fact that men began to make contracts, but came only when all men were free, or compelled, to make contracts. Consequently, at the time the greater part of goods was being distributed to ultimate consumers according to status, contracts of barter played a fairly important part in the distribution. Some men were free to make these contracts at practically all times, and from that practice money gradually evolved. The point of beginning is with that stage of society in which the great majority of people were attached to the land, or in some manner under the complete dominance of a ruler upon whom their status made them dependent for a living. He gave them such "subsistence" only as would enable them to work, "conveniences and amusements" being almost entirely lacking. They made no contracts. Princes, priests, and a few wealthy merchants made all the contracts.

The fact that men who by some means were able to become merchants made the great majority of contracts in such a society is indicated by the high stage of development reached in ancient times by maritime law and the law merchant. Both were then practically as good as any modern system of the kind, and indeed the general principles of those ancient laws remain in effect to-day. It was out of the Law Merchant that money developed.

Going back to the hand-to-hand exchanges of goods, it is to be observed that, when confidence and custom began to result in the formation of contracts involving some element of delayed performance, every article was capable of being used for two general purposes. One was for consumption, and the other as a means of acquiring things of a different kind. "To take, *e.g.,* a shoe, there is its use as a covering of the foot, and also its use as an article of exchange . . . This (latter) use arose in the first instance from natural circumstances, as people had more of some things and fewer of others than

15

they required." [6] Something more was necessary, however, to make a bridge across the gaps in time and space which arose from the delay in performance by the party whose promise of future delivery, perhaps at another place, was accepted as an exchange for immediate delivery by the other party. Naturally the disposition of a trader was to confine his acceptance of promises of future delivery — in exchange for the immediate transfer of his goods — to those commodities for which he knew he could find a market. Also, that market had to extend beyond any one place, as a limited market was subject to destruction by war, pestilence, and other calamities. The attention of such traders would naturally turn to the precious metals, which were in demand at all times and in all places. Furthermore, a stated quantity of metal of a certain standard of purity would be the same thing when delivered as when promised. It made for certainty, as no element of judgment was involved in the determination of its acceptability as a performance of the contract. The quantity could be determined by weighing, and the purity tested with an ever-increasing degree of accuracy.

[6] Aristotle, "Politics", Book I, Ch. IX.

Thus it seems probable that the most important use of the precious metals in commerce began as an innovation resorted to by merchants in an effort to achieve both convenience and certainty in the performance of contracts. Although the facts that the metals could be measured, subdivided, tested for quality, and transported with more ease and safety and less loss than other things made them serve the purpose of a medium of exchange, it is doubtful whether that was the manner in which their extensive use in commerce came about. The merchants made large transactions, and made them frequently: the common people made small transactions only and very few of those. There was little need for the merchants to subdivide the metals for use in their transactions, and when subdivided into pieces small enough for everyday transactions the pieces would be altogether too little for practical use. Perhaps this fact — that the merchants used the precious metals for large transactions — is one of the sources of the prejudice of the common people against the monetary use of gold. Certainly the belief that the monetary uses of the precious metals began as a medium of immediate exchange has been responsible for many fallacies in the discussion of money, and many mistakes in the legislation of all countries on the subject.

These contracts for future delivery of the precious metals offered an open way for the development of another innovation by means of which trade could be expanded. A merchant sending goods from one place to another in exchange for a promise to deliver a precious metal could direct the merchant for whom the goods were destined to deliver the metal to a third one. From that third merchant, the sender of the goods could obtain other goods not procurable from the second merchant. At times the one sending the goods would desire no goods in return, but wished to receive the metal. He could then try to find another merchant in his city who wished to obtain goods from the city for which his goods were destined. If successful he could exchange his goods for metal in his own city. As trade between the two cities grew, perhaps the merchant sending goods simply gave the leader of the transporting caravan, or captain of the ship, an order for delivery of metal drawn on the receiver of the goods. Then a merchant who wished to obtain goods from the other city, without sending metal away so much in advance of the time when he would receive the goods, could arrange, through the captain of the vessel as an intermediary, with the first merchant to use the metal to become due him.

By the time the practices of trade had reached the point at which a merchant in one city would order goods from one in another city, the way was open for bills of exchange to begin their work. At first the heads of caravans and captains of ships were probably merchants on their own account, taking goods from one place to barter for those in another place. This method of trading did not disappear with the advent of bills of exchange; but the use of the metals undoubtedly tended to cause those with merchandising instincts to see greater opportunities for profit by specializing in trade and getting out of the arduous tasks and risks of transportation. An order from one merchant to another for delivery of goods included also a promise to deliver metal in exchange for the goods. This promise to deliver metal became, by the custom of merchants, transferable, from the one to whom it was made to a merchant who desired to import goods from the city in which resided the merchant who had made the promise. Let it be assumed that merchant A in Babylon sent to merchant B in Orchoë an order for certain goods and a promise to give for them so many pieces of silver of a known standard of weight and fineness. At the same time merchant C in Babylon desired to acquire a different kind of goods from merchant D in Orchoë, and was looking for a means of making delivery in Orchoë of the necessary metal. Perhaps the promise of metal to B exceeded slightly the amount needed by C, but he was willing to have an excess of metal delivered to D, as there was constant trade between them. B then writes on his document from A an assignment to C of the promise to deliver silver, and C in turn writes on it an order that the metal be delivered to D. A bill of exchange was then an unconditional order in writing addressed by one merchant to another, signed by the one giving it, and requiring the one to whom it was addressed to deliver on demand, or at a fixed future time, a certain weight of a precious metal of a given fineness.

An actual bill of exchange, drawn between the two cities named above and fully developed as such, is set out in a most interesting and valuable little book on the Law Merchant.[7]

[7] W. A. Bewes, "The Romance of the Law Merchant", p. 50. (London, 1923, Sweet & Maxwell, Ltd.)

"Four minae fifteen shekels of silver (credit) of Ardu-
Nana, son of Yakin, on Mardukabalussur, son of Mardukbalatirib in the town of Orchoë, Mardukbalatirib will
pay in the month of Tebet four minae fifteen shekels of
silver to Belabaliddin, son of Sinnaid, Our the fourteenth
Arakhsamna, Second year of Nabu-nâhid, King of Babylon."

(The names of the witnesses follow.)

The expansion of trade among merchants had to
be accompanied by their dealings with greater and
greater numbers of the populace. As a given country
had more goods to enjoy, a large proportion of the
inhabitants would become able to enjoy them, and
hence free to make contracts. Perhaps the course
of development was an extension of the contracts
which the merchants made to furnish supplies to
wealthy owners of great herds of cattle, or large
agricultural estates, to retail transactions with the
populace of the cities. Confidence and custom could
be relied upon for the making of promises for future
performance in this kind of transaction as well as
in those among merchants only. The merchants had
been keeping records of promises to deliver the precious metals, the unit of account being a weight of
metal. Probably as a result of the extension of such

contracts and accounts to smaller transactions the weight used as a unit of account became a smaller one. That could lead to the actual making of bars, or ingots, of metal of that weight, and the passing of such pieces from hand to hand. It seems that here is where the use of a metal as a medium of exchange came in, as it is known that both contracts for future delivery of the metals and bills of exchange were in use long before any kind of coins appeared.[8] The importance of coins has been greatly exaggerated, and significance is to be given the view that the arrangement for the smaller transactions, in which coins were used, grew out of the arrangements for the larger transactions.

Now each time a metal was offered, either in an exchange or in discharge of a promise to deliver it, there was the necessity of weighing and testing it. This was inconvenient in small transactions, and perhaps some ingenious merchant, who noticed that he was constantly receiving the same pieces of metal, decided to save time and trouble by stamping some pieces with his own certificate of weight and fineness. This offers a suggestion as to what might have been the occasion of the official assumption of

[8] *Ibid.*

coinage by a ruler, or government. It is, of course, made in the absence of any historical record, and speculative only.

By the time stamped bars of metal were placed in circulation by merchants, governments had undoubtedly reached a stage of development where, to some extent, they enforced contracts. In order to enforce them their meaning had to be determined. It is rather difficult to conceive now of the actual cases which might have arisen for decision by such courts as there were in those days. Ideas which today are taken for granted may have been those of the radicals of that time. Let it be supposed, however, that a case came up for decision with the facts as follows:

A was given certain goods by B in return for A's promise to deliver on a certain date so many pieces of metal stamped by the merchant C as being each one-tenth part of a pound of silver nine tenths fine. A delivers the pieces so stamped, and B takes them to a merchant who refuses to trust the certificate stamped on the metal. Upon weighing and testing, the pieces are found to be one-twelfth part of a pound of silver each, and only eight tenths pure. B demands that A deliver pieces of metal which are actually of the weight and fineness stamped, as agreed. A answers that the pieces of the merchant C were in general circulation in the community, that no person had previously refused to accept pieces so stamped by C, and that the promise was to deliver a certain number of such pieces without any stipulation as to what the pieces should be in actual weight and quality.

The judge construes the contract according to A's contention, that he had delivered what he had promised to deliver. That makes B a loser, and he and his friends raise a hue and cry against the dishonest practices of the merchants. Everyone begins to weigh and test all such stamped pieces of metal before accepting them. Some cases of fraudulent stamping are discovered, and many cases of honest mistakes due to inaccuracies in the scales. As is usual in such cases, all the victims, and the reformers who join them, demand that the government forbid the merchants to stamp pieces of metal for circulation, and take over the business itself.

This suggests that the occasion of governmental interference may have been abuses by the merchants of their privilege of stamping pieces of metal with certificates of weight and fineness. There are two

24

other possible reasons for action by government with respect to circulating metal which should be considered. One was jealousy of the exercise of such a privilege by the merchants. Another was that promises to deliver metal may have become so prevalent that a change in conditions of trade brought about an agitation for what is known to-day as debtor's relief.

The nature of the privilege of stamping metal pieces for circulation must be thoroughly understood. To a certain extent this practice of the merchants was usurpation of a governmental function. They were certifying the weight and quality of a commodity, and it might have been argued with reason that the certification should be official. So to stamp the circulating metals was a privilege exercised by the merchants upon sufferance of government, and they could not demand its continuance as of right. By taking the privilege away from them the government simply became the official weigher and tester of a commodity, its function at this stage being more that of a keeper of weights and measures than of a creator of money. There could not have been any conscious thought on the part of anyone that money was being created by this step, and it is a great mistake so to regard it. Whatever government first undertook to stamp metal for circulation, or to strike coin, did no more than extend somewhat its rôle of umpire over the making and performance of contracts.

If governmental coinage resulted from an agitation for relief of those who had promised to deliver more metal than they could obtain without sacrificing all that they had, here again there would have been no more than an extension of the rôle of umpire over contracts. It seems improbable, however, that coinage by government was caused by such a movement, as the great majority of people were not making contracts at that stage of development.

The point to be emphasized is that however the power of government came to be applied to the use of pieces of metal as *media* of the exchanges, it was the power over contracts, to interpret and enforce them, which was exercised. Metals, in the form of coins, still circulated as commodities, although they bore an official certificate of weight and fineness. Commerce was still barter, although its conduct had been made much more convenient. Promises to pay money had not yet come into being, so far as legal contemplation is concerned: there were only promises to deliver metal.

When coinage was taken over by government, the unit of weight used by the merchants as a unit of account did not become the unit of coinage. Such a coin would have been far too valuable for the ordinary purposes of circulation. Some evidence on this is available from the fact that many historical units of account, which later became units of money — among others the pound sterling, the French livre, and the German mark — were originally a pound of silver.[9] Even if in the more ancient times to which reference is here made the unit of account was no more than a pound of silver, with silver then exchanging for gold at an approximate ratio of one to ten, that would have made such a unit worth more than forty dollars when compared with present-day prices. So the unit of coinage was made only a fraction of the unit of weight in which the merchants kept their accounts, and they continued to follow their own methods of accounting.

This provides further evidence that the arrangements for the smaller transactions grew out of those

[9] Feaveryear, "The Pound Sterling", pp. 7, 333. (Oxford University Press, 1931.)

which the merchants had developed for their larger transactions. Its importance lies in the facts that the merchants had worked out a method of doing business, their intention being to accomplish certain purposes, which they did very successfully; and that governments took over control of the same arrangements when their intention was, or at least should have been, to accomplish a set of purposes which were of a nature vastly different. A sharp contrast is to be made between the intention of the merchants to facilitate trade, and what came to be the intention of governments, which was to take toll from that trade. In other words, the interest of the merchants lay in preserving a system for the determination of contractual relations arising out of exchanges: but the interest of governments lay in providing a system for the collection of taxes. The merchants knew what they needed, and how to provide for it. Governments, however, neither saw their own wants clearly, nor understood how to accomplish their satisfaction, but foolishly tried to use for their purposes arrangements which had been developed for something else. The exchanges of the merchants passed beyond the boundaries of any particular country, being as wide in scope as the known world, but the collection of taxes was a matter for each individual country. All through history the purposes and understanding of the merchants conflict with the purposes and lack of comprehension of governments. It is necessary to keep constantly in mind this problem of providing for mercantile exchanges at the same time that provision is made for the collection of taxes. Apparently the world has known only one statesman, Alexander Hamilton, who recognized the problem and stated its solution.

Assuming that the name of the weight-account unit was "pound", the legal question of whether the meaning of a contract was to deliver so many "pounds" of the metal used for the exchanges, or to pay so many units of coinage, could not arise for decision by a court so long as both remained the same. But the largest coins struck by the government were not "pounds", being no more than fixed fractions of that. Let those coins be called "ounces." The law of coinage was that an ounce should contain a certain fraction, say one twelfth, of a pound of silver of a certain standard of fineness. Under those circumstances a contract for the sale of goods would have been made by acceptance of an offer to give so many "pounds" for the goods.

Now suppose the government decrees that henceforth each ounce coined, instead of containing one twelfth of a pound of silver, shall contain one twentieth of a pound of silver, but leaves that part of the law which says that twelve ounces make a "pound" unchanged. The weight-account unit and the unit of coinage still have the same name, but are no longer the same thing. Then arises the legal question of whether the contract to give "pounds" for goods is to be interpreted as meaning the unit of weight or the unit of coinage in using the term "pounds."

As to the intended meaning of the parties there can be little doubt. Their intention was to specify delivery of a pound of metal by weight, in a certain standard of fineness. The interest of the government, however, was directly to the contrary; and it was both the creator of the coin and the declarer of the law of contracts. It had the power to specify what amount of metal the coin should contain, and the power to declare the meaning of all terms used in a contract, even if the parties had intended to exclude the very meaning so prescribed. Perhaps the necessities of the government had made it seem appropriate so to debase the coinage in order that it might meet its expenses with more ease.

The custom and the law came to be that a promise to deliver coins by name could be discharged by delivery of whatever coin was issued by the government and given that name. So long as there was coined money only, and that made of the precious metals, this rule was of little importance except at the particular times when there happened to be a debasement of the coinage. Later it became of more importance, but that was after complete development of contracts to deliver the metals in the form of coins. Sometimes debasement of the coinage was secret and fraudulent in intent, as was the case under some of the later Roman Emperors; and at others it was simply an announced debasement to a coin of lesser metallic content, which remained fixed for a long period.

It seems that in ancient times there was some use of copper for making coins of smaller denominations, but there is no direct evidence of any arrangements by which there could be maintained a fixed rate of exchange between such copper coins and those of silver or gold. Such an arrangement in modern nations is made through a system of token coinage, but that was so little understood that it was not adopted in England until 1816, and in the United States not until 1853. Where in former times copper coins circulated along with silver, perhaps merchants exchanged the two at the current market ratio of exchange between the two metals.[10]

[10] Alexander Del Mar, an interesting but very unconventional writer on money, contended that the iron money of the Spartans was really a wisely created and well-regulated system of token coinage; that the iron pieces were deliberately made useless — by being boiled in vinegar, he says; and that gold and silver were treated as ordinary commodities to be bought and sold by means of the iron money. He made the same contention with respect to the copper coinage of the Romans, and adduced some supporting evidence for that. See his "Money and Civilization." An explanation of the adoption of silver coinage by the Romans, and the primary cause of the abandonment of their token copper coinage, he gave in "The Science of Money" (Macmillan, 1896), p. 38: —

In A.U.C. 369 the Romans adopted a nummulary system copied from the Greeks, and based on 'principles of equity': in A.U.C. 406 they first began to allow pay to their troops; and as the latter had often to purchase their supplies, luxuries, or favors, in districts or from peoples among whom the nummularies had no currency, it was deemed necessary to pay them in silver coins.

Del Mar's reasoning was all based upon the erroneous premise that the function of money is to measure value, and he neglected commerce among nations almost completely. His works are worth reading, however, both for valuable information and general interest.

The development considered so far has been strictly that of a system of private contracts. There has been no progress beyond barter. The rôle of governments has been largely confined to stamping pieces of metal with official certificates of weight and fineness. Extensions of that rôle of governments must now be given consideration, in broad outlines over a long lapse of time.

Ancient empires were extensive, the greater ones covering the known and developed area of trade. Traffic beyond the limits of such empires was mostly pure barter with half-civilized tribes. The Roman Empire was a lawgiver which for centuries enabled contracts to be made and safely performed throughout the world then known as civilized. There was, however, a complete failure of the Romans to understand either the mercantile process of distributing goods or the collection of taxes. The Emperors even reverted to the collection of taxes in kind, and the Roman armies were frequently quartered on, as well as fed by, the provinces within which they were stationed.[11] This inability to develop a system

[11] Rostovtzeff, "Social and Economic History of the Roman Empire", pp. 310, 339, 375, 462.

for the collection of taxes must have been one cause of the repeated debasements of the coinage by the later Emperors, which almost prevented the system of the merchants from operating. A promise to deliver metal was no longer dischargeable according to the custom of merchants, but debts incurred could be paid with debased Roman coins at legal tender values. These debasements are not to be regarded as causes of disintegration, however, but as the result of deterioration in government. The *Pax Romana,* which gave such a wide field of safety for commerce and industry and created real prosperity, did not succumb to violence on account of debasements of coinage, as they occurred for the same reason internal strife succeeded peace. There were no longer in the government the intelligence and the power necessary either to preserve peace or support a currency. World-wide prosperity lasted just as long as there was a stable, powerful, and intelligent government to maintain the conditions under which it could exist, and that prosperity passed away with the *Pax Romana.* Economic conditions do not cause currency debasement. Just as truly as "War is the breakdown of a statesman's policy", a government's debasement of its currency shows that it lacks stability, power, and intelligence — without the necessity of mentioning integrity.

Under such circumstances it seems idle to speculate on whether "the long stagnation of the Middle Ages may not have been more surely and inevitably caused by Europe's meager supply of the monetary metals than by monasticism or Gothic frenzy." [12] When there was good government the enterprise of men obtained the precious metals, and also to a great extent invented satisfactory substitutes for them. The fact that the maximum stock of the precious metals held by ancient Europe, which was reached in the time of Augustus, fell to one eleventh of that by A.D. 800 [13] is in this connection hardly more than an indication of the decline in the general character of government. A workable system is always evolved from the customs of merchants — when governments will give it an opportunity to work.

When the *Pax Romana* was succeeded first by the chaos of the barbarian invasions and later by the Feudal System, the lack of governmental protection prevented the performance of contracts. The

[12] Keynes, "A Treatise on Money", Vol. II, p. 151.
[13] *Ibid.*

risk of making them was too great, as piracy and robbery restrained all commerce.[14] Men, even those who were free to enter into such relations, could no longer be employed to perform contracts, and many reverted to a condition of *status* by coming under the dominance of some powerful nobleman and being attached to his land. Development of the process had to begin all over again, and it was not until the time of the Crusades that Western Europe re-established familiarity with the custom of merchants.[15] The strength of the Law Merchant is forcibly contrasted with the weakness of governments in the fact that it may almost be said that the itinerant merchants carried their own courts with them from country to country. In each Mediæval Fair, the great places of trade in those times, there was established a court of *"pie poudre"* in which the Law Merchant was in effect declared by merchants.[16] A real revival of the

[14] W. Cunningham, "Growth of English Industry and Commerce" (5th Ed.), Vol. I, 51, 300–304. Cambridge University Press, 1910.

[15] "The Romance of the Law Merchant", pp. 2, 109.

[16] This is not to say that the merchants presided over the courts or enforced the judgments. Lipson's "Economic History of England", p. 225, explains this as follows: —

The president of the court was the mayor or bailiffs of the borough, or the steward where the franchise was not under municipal

monetary process did not occur until governments once more became powerful and intelligent enough to have courts of their own which were capable of understanding and applying the Law Merchant.[17] The rise of those governments had most important effects upon the manner in which the monetary process was conducted.

---

control. With the president, who executed the judgment of the court, was associated a varying number of assessors who helped to administer justice, and in cases affecting alien merchants half of them were drawn from aliens present at the fair. These assessors were themselves merchants, and in accordance with mediæval procedure they were the suitors who gave the verdict, and — whenever difficulties arose — declared the law. There was commonly, though not invariably, an appeal from their judgment to the supreme courts. The competence of the court covered a great variety of pleas arising from debts, contracts, trespasses, breaches of the assizes of bread, and ale.

The functions of the merchant assessors seem to have been to advise the president of the court as to the application of the Law Merchant to the facts in the case. ("To every fair is of right pertaining a court of piepowder." Coke's "Institutes," II, p. 220.) The point is that governments had not judges of their own capable of applying the Law Merchant.

[17] Lord Mansfield, who was Chief Justice in England from 1756 to 1788, is generally credited with introducing into the English Common Law System, which was poorly adapted to the usages of commerce, enough of the Law Merchant to develop a more workable system. For an excellent discussion of some commercial aspects of the Common Law with particular reference to the reasons for its not being suitable for commerce in 1756 see Edward A. Adler, "Business Jurisprudence", 28 *Harvard Law Review,* p. 135.

It is probable that the low point in quality of government was reached some time prior to the checking of the tide of Mohammedan conquests in Europe by Charles Martel's victory at the Battle of Tours in 732. For some centuries after that, efforts to re-establish an empire co-extensive with the European boundaries of the Roman Empire thwarted instead of aided a revival in government, although Charlemagne did make some progress in that direction. Great significance must be given the fact that these attempts at the re-establishment of a European Empire failed, and that the revival of government, when it finally came, was along the line of separate nationalities. The one great trade area of the *Pax Romana* was split up into territories occupied by many small semi-nationalities. Some of these monarchies gradually developed governments of sufficient power and intelligence to bring comparatively large areas under a "King's Peace" in which commerce and industry might be safely conducted once more.

The rise of these governments is not to be ascribed to economic factors, except as a renewal of commercial contacts brought more knowledge out of the East. Probably the revival of learning was much more a cause of governments' becoming able to prevent piracy and robbery, and thereby becoming able to give men a chance to make commitments in enterprises which required the employment of other men, than a revival of prosperity was a cause of good government. The gold and silver which came in as a result of the discovery of America were not nearly so much a cause of prosperity as was the fact that Ferdinand and Isabella had succeeded in establishing a government powerful enough to send out an expedition to make the discovery. Spain might have been a wealthy and powerful nation for a much longer time had her government continued to be intelligent; but its decline in intelligence soon caused an almost complete loss of power. The combination of stability, power, and intelligence in a government, which in turn creates integrity, appeared in England to an extent greater than in any other country.

Roman ignorance of methods of providing for the collection of taxes was a heritage of the new national governments which sprang up in Europe. In many countries the monarchs of mediæval times depended upon revenues from private estates, instead of upon taxation. Naturally when they finally came to levy taxes, one of the methods to which they resorted was that of taking toll from the things of commerce which passed where they could be grasped. Thus when they established mints they attempted to collect a seigniorage charge as toll out of the precious metals brought in for coinage. Governments had not, of course, reached the point at which they could provide any kind of monetary substitute for the precious metals as a means of paying taxes, and the collection of seigniorage charges really tended to impair the ability of the people to do business as well as to pay taxes. Sometimes the governments would acquire precious metal and coin it, but mostly for the creation of money they depended on the desire of merchants for coin to bring the metals to the mints, which impulse was restrained by the necessity of paying seigniorage. Each country had a different weight of metal as its unit of coinage, which was the first factor in beginning to create the great, and all-important, distinction between the internal circulation of money in these nations and the circulation of the precious metals.[18]

[18] To go forward in time, for an illustration of the consequences of the failure of statesmen to understand the nature of this distinction: It shows one reason for the ineffectiveness of devaluation of the dollar in 1933 as a means of raising internal prices. The dollar, which was required as the means of paying to

No sooner did the varying coins issue from these national mints than they became subject to the clipper and "sweater" as well as to loss of weight from natural wear and tear. For these reasons it was almost impossible to keep good coins in circulation. Even the depreciated coins were good in payment of taxes, however, until they reached a state of great loss of weight, and they were also good in the payment of private debts.[19] In causing this distinction between the internal circulation of money and the circulation of the precious metals, there were at work at the same time both the collection of taxes and the principle of "legal tender." A legal tender may be defined as an offer of payment in a kind of money which must be accepted by the one to

the national, state, and local municipal governments nearly nine thousand millions in taxes per year, to say nothing of its legal-tender uses in the payment of internal private debts, was something entirely different from its so-called "gold content" of 23.22 grains of pure gold. Furthermore, a direct result of the lack of comprehension of this distinction is the fallacious "gold reserve" theory of creating paper money, which Great Britain through bitter experience learned to abandon as early as 1844, following the example of Alexander Hamilton in rejecting it, and to which the United States reverted with its Federal Reserve Act in 1913, to the great disaster of its own people as well as those of the entire world. The subject is well worthy of attention.

[19] Lipson's "Economic History of England", p. 512.

whom it is offered in payment of a debt, or when the one to whom it is offered is under a duty to render a service upon such a tender being made; the consequences of refusing acceptance in the first instance being that the debt ceases to draw interest, and in the second that a legal liability for damages is incurred. Here is the cause of the operation of what is known as Sir Thomas Gresham's Law, — that bad money drives out good money, — which seems, however, to have been recognized as anciently as in "The Frogs" of Aristophanes.[20] When worn, or clipped, coins were accepted by the sovereign in payment of taxes, and were by law of obligatory acceptance in the discharge of debts; such coins naturally had an internal "purchasing power" in excess of that of the precious metal which they contained.

[20] Del Mar pointed this out: —

Often has it crossed my fancy, that the city loves to deal
With the very best and noblest members of her commonweal,
Just as with our ancient coinage, and the newly-minted gold.
Yea, for these, our sterling pieces, all of pure Athenian mold,
All of perfect die and metal, all the fairest of the fair,
All of workmanship unequaled, proved and valued everywhere
Both amongst our own Hellenes and Barbarians far away,
These we use not: but the worthless pinchbeck coins of yester-
day,
Vilest die and basest metal, now we always use instead.

— From B. B. Rogers' translation, in "Harvard Classics."

Consequently, anyone who had a payment to make in another country would not send there a precious metal in the form of worn coins, to sell for the money of that other country, but would endeavor to obtain for the purpose either full weight coins or metal in bullion form. Although the laws of the various countries generally forbade the exporting of precious metals, either as coins or bullion, shipments were constantly made surreptitiously.

The appearance of money is thus made to depend upon the exercise of a national taxing power. Not so much importance is to be ascribed to the law of legal tender, as the means of paying taxes is not always a means of discharging debts. For an instance of that: While in the United States National Bank notes and Federal Reserve notes were not legal tender until 1933, they were a means of paying most taxes to the Government itself. The principle was stated, possibly for the first time, by Alexander Hamilton, as follows: —

To designate or appoint the *money* or *thing* in which taxes are to be paid, is not only a proper but a *necessary exercise* of the power of collecting them. Accordingly Congress, in the law concerning the collection of the duties on imports and tonnage, have provided that they shall be paid in gold and silver. But while it was an indispensable part of the work to say in what they should be paid, the choice of the specific thing was mere matter of discretion. The payment might have been required in the commodities themselves. Taxes in kind, however ill-judged, are not without precedents, even in the United States; or it might have been in the paper money of the several states, or in the bills of the banks of North America, New York, and Massachusetts, all or either of them; or it might have been in bills issued under the authority of the United States.

No part of this can, it is presumed, be disputed. The appointment, then, of the *money* or *thing* in which the taxes are to be paid, is an incident to the power of collection. And among the expedients which may be adopted, is that of bills issued under the authority of the United States.[21]

Therefore, it seems that the correct definition of money is that it is anything which a sovereign, national government declares to be receivable in the payment of taxes which it levies.[22] Money thus appears to be purely a national instrument, and "a

[21] Letter to President Washington on the Constitutionality of the Bank of the United States, "Hamilton's Papers on Public Credit, Commerce and Finance", edited by Samuel McKee, Jr., Columbia University Press, p. 123.

[22] Georg Friedrich Knapp, "The State Theory of Money", p. 95. (Macmillan & Co., Ltd., London, 1924.) Knapp speaks of "State Acceptance" without relating it definitely to taxation.

creature of law." [23] It is to be noticed that money created on this principle does not become *fiat* money until the government which creates it either announces that it will discharge its own indebtedness with such money, or that such money must be received in discharge of private debts, or both. The first of these steps is entirely natural, and can do no harm so long as the government is intelligent enough to know that it cannot create money for the purpose of paying its own bills, and that the sole purpose of its creating it at all is that taxes may be paid to it on a just basis. So far as commerce and industry are concerned, they would work out a far better process for their purposes if governments created no money. But the necessity of collecting taxes, and the great extensions of the taxing power in modern times, demand the creation of money by governments. It should be done with a clear recognition of its relation to the taxing power, of the extent to which the exercise of the latter power determines the extent to which the power to create money may be exercised, and of the fact that, although money itself does not cross national borders, the monetary process is world-wide in scope. When principles are

[23] *Ibid.*, p. 1.

developed in accordance with these facts, the creation of money for the purpose of collecting taxes offers a far stronger check on the abuse of monetary powers by governments than any self-imposed gold reserve requirement may ever supply. This principle, recognized and successfully used by Alexander Hamilton and finally worked out by experience in Great Britain without any very clear exposition of why it was completely adopted in 1844, must be studied in the light of its development in national monetary laws of the two countries. Before that is considered, it seems advisable to pursue a little further the subject of the circulation of money as distinguished from the circulation of the precious metals.

As has been observed in the first part of this chapter, in ancient times bills of exchange began to have a limited circulation as a kind of physical evidence of the existence of a contract to deliver a stated quantity of metal. Those ancient bills of exchange were the origin of both the bank note and the modern check. The bill of exchange was an order drawn by one person upon another for the delivery of metal, in bullion or coin, and was the representation of the drawer that a contract existed.

It was easy enough to change the form of the physical evidence of the existence of such a contract from the signed statement of the one to whom the promise of delivery had been made to the signed statement of the promissor. That was done when, for the convenience of small transactions, it was desirable to have the statement of a well-known and wealthy person that he had made a promise to deliver metal, and the bank note was the result. The extensive circulation of bank notes as evidences of contracts to deliver a precious metal, and in a form which could be conveniently transferred from one person to another, offered to governments an irresistible temptation. They began to make such contracts to deliver the precious metals.

The government official who started this practice gave to the world an unmitigated curse. It was no part of the business of governments to engage in dealing in precious metals. The making of contracts to deliver metals had been begun by merchants, not as a separate business, but as a means of facilitating comparatively large transactions involving the exchange of goods, to which the practice was admirably suited. Then the practice was extended to the facilitation of small retail transactions — for which it was less suitable, but would work so long as governments did not engage in the making of such contracts. The purposes of such contracts when of a commercial nature must be sharply contrasted with the purposes for which governments made them.

A merchant's contract to deliver a precious metal was made because he either had it or expected to acquire it and wished to dispose of it for other goods. A government's contract of the same kind was made because it did not have the metal and wished to create something which it could use instead of metal. The folly of basing systems of taxation and of internal distribution of goods on any such perversion of the nature of a mercantile instrument should have been apparent to any statesman.

Some governments followed the practice of issuing for circulation their own promises to deliver metal, the quantities being stated in terms of their coinage units, and others established banks to serve their purposes in this respect. In the latter cases the governments would make their contracts to deliver metal to the bank, and the bank would issue to the public its promises to deliver metal on demand. The greater part of the metal promised was not in existence and could not be produced by either the government or its bank, but this defect was supposed to be remedied by the keeping of a metallic reserve out of which such promises could be redeemed. The full significance of the fact that such promises could not circulate in foreign countries was completely overlooked. That was due to the fact that their value depended, not upon the amount of metal by which they were supposed to be secured, but upon the demand for such promises as a means of paying taxes to the government which had caused them to be issued. The failure to make the quantity of these promises depend upon the extent to which the taxing power was being used, instead of upon a fluctuating supply of metal, had disastrous consequences.

The use of these government-sanctioned promises to deliver metal set up an additional disturbing variation of the internal circulation of money, different from that of the precious metals, which was largely international. Such notes usually had an internal purchasing power which was less than that of the amount of metal represented. Also the supply of money fluctuated with the supply of metal, or at least was supposed to do so. The consequences of this must be considered with reference to both the payment of taxes and the internal distribution of goods.

It is perfectly clear that no national government should let the amount it collects in taxes be dependent upon, or vary with, the amount of a precious metal which is held either by its own agencies, including both its Treasury and a central bank, or within its borders. When the gold reserve principle of issuing notes is followed, a government permits the supply of the means of paying taxes to vary with the supply of the metal called for by the notes. Thus, when the metal departs to an extent which demands a decrease in the note issue, it becomes as difficult to pay taxes as if the rate had been suddenly raised; for the law is that the reserve must be maintained by decreasing the supply of the means of paying taxes. The demand for the notes for the purpose of paying taxes remains the same. On the other hand, if the supply of metal increases the supply of notes increases, it becomes easier to pay taxes, and the government really gets less. So, in effect, this system does result in a government's allowing the amount of actual wealth it takes in the form of taxes to vary with the supply of metal. In modern nations, which collect such great amounts of taxes, that is disturbance enough; but the disturbance which this fluctuation causes in the distribution of goods is even greater.

The part of a nation's production of goods which is consumed by the operating expenses of its government may be regarded as the setting aside of one share in those goods, which is measured, in quantity but not in value, by the amount of money which the government collects in taxes. Just as the government's money income measures the share of national production which it may consume, so does the income in money of every citizen measure the share which he may have of available "subsistence, conveniences, and amusements." The contracts which he has made, whether for interest, dividends, wages, or a salary, determine the amount of money he will receive in the course of a year. These contracts are not subject to changes on account of fluctuations in the supply of metal, unless their obligation is impaired, but the share which the money will allot is subject to change on that account. Thus a variation in the share of the government is accompanied by, and intensifies, a variation in the share of the citizen, from which at times he may benefit and at others suffer acutely.

This system of making contracts to deliver metal the means both of paying taxes and of discharging private contracts introduced a speculative element which was not so disturbing when only wealthy and powerful men made contracts. They knew how to appraise the risks attendant upon the expansions and contractions of the metallic base of credit to an extent far greater than inexperienced workers having small capital. The latter had been more dependent upon the wealth, power, and skill of their head men than upon their own efforts. The situation was changed entirely, however, when the Industrial Revolution took men away from the land and made everyone, except some farmers, dependent for a livelihood upon the performance of contracts to pay money.[24]

Not only did the number of men who made con-

[24] W. Cunningham, "Growth of English Commerce and Industry", Vol. 3, p. 616: —

The divorce of the industrial population from the soil tended on the one hand to the impoverishment of the rural districts, from which manufactures were withdrawn, and on the other to a notable change in the position of the workman; he came to be wholly dependent on his earnings, and to have no other source to which he could look for support. The cottage weavers, whether wage-earners or independent

tracts increase enormously, but in addition to salary and wage contracts there came in long-term contracts for the payment of money, such as corporate bonds and mortgages of private persons. Debentures and stock certificates fall into somewhat the same class. Men who were dependent upon these various kinds of contracts for money with which to acquire their shares of "subsistence, conveniences, and amusements" saw the quantity of such things so obtainable constantly fluctuating. When prices were high the amount of money called for by their contracts would entitle them to less, and when prices were low the money payable by virtue of their contracts was likely to be reduced or not forthcoming at all. In many cases their contracts, in other words their jobs, were lost entirely.

Modern monetary systems are similar to the bar-

men, had had the opportunity of work in the fields in harvest and of supplementing their income from their gardens or through their privileges on the common wastes. When the industrial population was massed in factory towns, they were necessarily deprived of these subsidiary sources of income, and their terms of employment were affected by the state of trade. So long as cottage industry lasted, the workmen had something to fall back upon when times were bad; but under the new conditions the fluctuations were much more violent than they had ever been before, and the workman had no means of improving his position. The prosperity of the mass of the population no longer rested on the solid basis of land, but upon the fluctuating basis of trade.

ter of ancient and mediæval societies in that both are made to depend upon the use of precious metals. The metals are now used for three purposes which did not exist to any great extent when they were first introduced into the contractual system: long-term contracts, universal distribution by contract, and the collection of large sums in taxes.

As to long-term contracts: The metals were introduced for commercial transactions, which are always of comparatively short term so far as payments are concerned. Society never should have permitted them to be used as a means of discharging obligations becoming due at intervals over long periods of years. This is an unfortunate instance of the organization of society failing to keep up with changes in conditions, and of the ever-recurring attempts to use an old instrument for new purposes. The remedy lies, not in prohibiting the use of the instrument altogether, but in confining its use to the purposes which formerly it served so well: that is, under modern conditions contracts to deliver the precious metals should be confined to commercial exchanges in commerce among nations.

In a society organized largely on the basis of land

and status, the precious metals were not used to any great extent as the means of distributing goods, but instead mostly for exchanges which were only occasional for all men except those engaged in commerce. When the industrialization of society made it necessary to distribute goods through contracts and money to a great number of people, there was an urgent demand for any one of three changes: an increase in the supply of the precious metals; an improved organization of the means of making and performing contracts to deliver the precious metals; the use of something other than the precious metals as money. As the first was mostly beyond the control of men, the choice was confined to the second and third. The situation demanded a choice between the two — and not an attempt to use both, which was the mistake into which governments fell. By encouraging the development of banks they attempted to follow the first of the alternatives, and by declaring certain kinds of contracts to deliver the precious metals to be money they sought to take advantage of the second. The incompatibility of the two remedies appears readily enough from an examination of the way in which the system of distribution through contracts and money works in a system founded on the second alternative and in a combination of the second and third.

With a precious metal in full-value coins alone being money, — that is, the only means of paying taxes and making a legal tender, — the stock of goods available for distribution in a nation is to be regarded as in two parts, the first the precious metal used for coinage, and the second all other goods. Subdivisions of the metal part are used as a means of acquiring shares in the other part. As contracts to deliver the metal are given no artificial support by the government, the measurement of shares in consumable goods through the supply of metal is comparatively direct without the cumulative effect of any other instrument. If the supply of metal decreases, the share of consumable goods which will be measured out and distributed by a given amount of the metal merely increases in proportion. This fluctuation in the purchasing power of money will be comparatively easy to stand, even in an industrial nation, as there is neither the erection of a superstructure nor its collapse. With certain exceptions this was the situation in the United States at the time of the Panic, or Depression, of 1857 — and that was probably the mildest one we have ever had, which was attributable to the facts that the only forms of money were coined gold and token silver, and no contracts to deliver gold were either acceptable in payment of taxes to the National Government or a legal tender in private payments.

When contracts to deliver gold are made money by being acceptable in payment of taxes and usable as legal tender, the goods available for distribution in such a nation are still to be regarded as in two parts, one of gold and the second of all other goods. The gold alone no longer makes the distribution of the other part. There are two stocks distributable by means of all the money, which must rise and fall in supply with the stock of gold. Suppose, in an extreme case, the stock of gold is one thousand millions, the supply of money two-and-one-half thousand millions, and that the legal requirement is that the gold shall be forty per cent. of the money. A change in the gold stock is now given a cumulative effect. The superstructure of contracts to pay money is built up on the contracts to deliver gold, where in the first case there were only private contracts to pay money. Obviously the existence of such a superstructure causes more violent fluctuations in the shares of goods measurable by a given amount of money. The Depressions of 1837 and 1929 occurred in the United States under these circumstances, both being more severe than the one of 1857.

The solution of this problem to a reasonable extent, it being impossible as well as undesirable to prevent all such fluctuations, does not demand the abolition of contracts to deliver gold, or that there shall not be a fixed price for gold. It does demand, however, that governments stop dealing in gold, and permit it to be used for the original purpose of merchants in making contracts to deliver it. That requires a world-wide Standard of International Trade, which might conceivably be created independently of gold, but is not likely to be so created. Commerce among nations is barter, and for its proper facilitation gold must serve as a commodity which may be bought at a fixed price in one country and freely shipped to another country, there to be sold at a fixed price to obtain money for buying goods.

There is only one way that a fixed price for gold may be reasonably maintained, which is by means of the establishment and administration of a Standard of International Trade. Such a Standard consists of something more than each nation's having a fixed price for gold, and consideration of the subject should be approached with appreciation of the fact that in all the centuries since the Fall of the Roman Empire the only time there has been a real Standard for commerce among nations was during the period from 1846 until 1914. That Standard may be created and administered by the most powerful nation only, all that the others may do in that respect being to take advantage of its existence and to follow along. Little may the secondary nations aid in either the creation or the maintenance of the Standard.

There is another prerequisite to the existence of such a Standard, the fulfillment of which depends upon the most powerful nation exclusively. The Standard cannot be created unless that nation distinguishes between the internal circulation of its money and the circulation in commerce among nations of the precious metal the fixed price of which is a part of the arrangements set up for the operation of the Standard. One result of this is that the nation which creates the Standard and the monetary institutions for its administration must definitely operate upon the principle that its money is created by law without being subject to the automatic control of the standard precious metal. Only a government which stands pre-eminently above all others in stability, power, intelligence, and integrity, may even attempt this task.

From 1815 until 1914 Great Britain was the only nation which could undertake to fulfill this duty, and it took her thirty-one years to learn how to do it. Her experience during that period of trial and error shows that it is more dangerous for such a nation to refuse to assume the burden than it is to take the risk. To-day the United States is the only nation which may succeed in creating a Standard of International Trade, and is undergoing experiences which in many respects are comparable to those of Great Britain from 1815 to 1846.

The next three chapters are an inquiry into the evolution and nature of the principles upon which Great Britain achieved success to a reasonable degree.

CHAPTER II

MONETARY DEVELOPMENT IN ENGLAND

As Great Britain is the only nation which has ever
created and administered successfully a Standard
of International Trade, it is necessary to study the
course of monetary development in England from
the time of the beginning of the trend toward the
establishment of that Standard. The principles upon
which the Standard was finally created and administered were not deduced from any one theory as to
the nature of the monetary process, but were slowly
learned from experience. In fact, the knowledge of
correct principles was so slowly acquired in England
that Alexander Hamilton prepared for the United
States a far better set of monetary laws than those
which prevailed in England at the end of the eighteenth century. Hamilton acquired his knowledge
from English sources, and in order to consider the
principles which he adopted a general view of the
English background is required. Therefore this
chapter reviews in broad outline the course of devel-

opment of monetary laws in England from 1661 until 1791, the time Hamilton used his knowledge acquired from study of those laws and the facts connected with their operation.

It seems that the statesmen of "a nation of shopkeepers" recognized the fact that the making and performance of contracts furnished employment to men, and were a more important part of the monetary process than the striking of coin or the issuance of paper substitutes for the precious metals. The beginning in recognition of the necessity for freedom of contract began to take place about 1660, and a few years later received the accompaniment of a government which has remained stable from that time until the present. Before considering the course of that development, it is necessary to make a brief statement as to the nature of the monetary institutions of England as they were in the middle of the seventeenth century.

The pound sterling not only is the most famous monetary unit the world has ever known, but has been the longest lived and the most stable. There has been no coin to bear its name. Originally, the term "pound" was applied to two hundred and forty pennies coined from a pound of silver. That seems to go back to Anglo-Saxon times, when the pound was a weight-account unit probably of the merchants alone, as it was too large for use by the common people. The pennies began to be called "sterlings" in the first part of the twelfth century, and from that came the name "pound sterling." Silver of the sterling standard, an alloy 925 parts of pure silver in 1000, which was prescribed for the Mint in the Tower of London by William the Conqueror, was a recognized part of the commerce of mediæval Europe. Subdivisions of the pound sterling as an account unit, into fractions larger than pennies, resulted in shillings being coined as the equivalent of twelve silver pennies.

William the Conqueror, by adopting a pound some six per cent. lighter, seems to have begun a departure from what was probably the troy pound of silver as the weight-account unit described by the pound sterling. The coins representing fractions of the sterling unit of account were successively made lighter, until all reference to a pound of silver was almost forgotten. A great part of the cause of that is attributable to the fact that all coins were clipped and sweated as soon as issued, and when a recoinage became necessary it was frequently impossible to obtain enough silver to re-issue the coins in sufficient number at the old standard. By 1660 a standard pound of silver was coined into sixty-two shillings, which, with two shillings being deductible for seigniorage and expenses, made the metallic depreciation of the pound sterling at that time about two thirds. The money of England then consisted of silver shillings and copper pence, with the unit of account the pound sterling.[1] There had been, at various times, some efforts to put gold coins into circulation; but they were no more than a commodity, subject to fluctuating prices in pounds and shillings. The prevailing standard was distinctly one of silver, and it will be important later to observe how the shift was made to a gold standard.

Banking was not out of the hands of the goldsmiths by 1660. They began the development of banking in England, just as they did on the Continent of Europe. At first they had desired to get possession of coins so that they might sort out the better ones for export, in defiance of the law, and return the others to circulation. To obtain the coins

[1] The recital of facts made in this chapter is largely based upon, and much credit must be given to, Feaveryear's "The Pound Sterling", a most excellent and valuable work.

they offered to pay interest on money deposited with them, and it seems that the first coins actually so deposited were brought by stewards charged with the duty of keeping the money of wealthy landowners. The latter had developed the custom of paying bills by giving an order on their stewards, to whom the goldsmiths offered a safe place of storage. A receipt would be given for coins so deposited, and that would contain, or imply, a promise to repay, sometimes on demand and in other cases so many days after notice. As money was withdrawn a statement of the amount drawn out would be written on the back of the document. These receipts gradually evolved into documents bearing a promise to pay to the order of the depositor, and later, when they came to be bank notes, to the bearer. Also, to a limited extent, there was a use of written orders to the goldsmiths to pay money. Such practices hardly prevailed outside of London, and were there confined to dealings of the goldsmiths with noblemen and merchants. The goldsmiths solicited deposits from both classes, and by the middle of the seventeenth century were rapidly becoming bankers.

It is worth noting how much the profit of the goldsmiths — in the business of sorting out good coins, exporting them, and paying their bills, or notes, with the more debased coins — was dependent upon the observance of one law and the violation of another. The law of legal tender permitted them to pay their notes with worn and clipped coins, provided they were not defaced beyond all recognition. It seems that English coins had always passed by number and not by weight. At that time the export of both coins and bullion was forbidden by law, but the goldsmiths habitually violated this prohibition.

The fact that for centuries there had always been in England some collection of taxes in money was of importance. Lipson's "Economic History of England" quotes a twelfth-century account of a great change in the system of taxation as follows: —

"According to the tradition handed down to us by our fathers, in the early state of the kingdom after the Conquest, the kings used to receive from their manors not sums of gold or silver but only provisions, from which were supplied the daily necessaries of the king's household. . . . This system then prevailed during the whole reign of King William I, and down to the time of King Henry his son; so that I have myself met people who have seen provisions brought to the court at appointed times from the royal manors." An allowance was made for these to the sheriff. "But as time went on, when King Henry was engaged abroad or in remote parts of the country in suppressing rebellion, it became necessary that he should have coined money for his expenditure. And at the same time there poured into the King's court crowds of complaining husbandmen, or — what was more disagreeable to him — often met him as he journeyed, holding up their ploughshares as a sign that agriculture was decaying. . . . Accordingly the king, moved by their complaints, acting on the advice of his magnates, sent through the kingdom men whom he knew to be wise and fitted for the work, in order that they might visit and inspect each manor with their own eyes and then estimate in money the value of the payments in kind. And they arranged that the sheriff of the county should be responsible at the Exchequer for the total amount due from all the manors in the shire." [2]

It seems that bad coins could be used to pay the sheriff but not by him to pay the King. As the sheriff was charged with the taxes levied within the territory for which he was responsible, probably he had to accept whatever coins were offered.

A real system of taxation was only beginning to be developed in the middle of the seventeenth century. Until the supremacy of Parliament was established by the Puritan Revolution and confirmed by the one in 1688, Parliament regarded all taxes,

[2] Lipson, "The Economic History of England", p. 515.

except custom duties at the ports, as grants of subsidies to the Crown to aid it in paying the expenses of government with the income from Crown property.[8] After 1688, however, both expenditures and taxes came under the control of Parliament, and what was probably the best system of taxation in the world was gradually created.

What occurred in England with respect to money and banking during the years from 1661 until the end of that century gave direction to the monetary history of the world as well as to that of England. The first important event was the beginning of freedom of trade in the precious metals. Charles II began to grant licenses to export bullion, and that brought about a statute which permitted gold and silver to be exported in any form except that of English coin. That was part of an Act of Parliament in 1663, appropriately entitled "An Act for the Encouragement of Trade." Foreign coin, or bullion, could thus be sent into England with an assurance that if its investment did not prove profitable what was left could be brought out again.

[8] For some interesting comments on the significance of these facts, see Hilaire Belloc's "Charles I, King of England", pp. 25. 36.

Coinage was encouraged by the introduction in 1663 of the milled coin, the well-marked edges of which prevented clipping. The Government could obtain little silver to coin, however, and the seigniorage and expense charges generally prevented silver from going to the Mint. The invention of the milled coin was of great importance in that it offered the hope of keeping full-weight coins in circulation. Although that hope was destined to disappointment, as the goldsmiths evidently knew it would be, it contributed to significant results. The merchants desired more money, and the goldsmiths were not averse to full-weight coins being put into circulation, believing that they could still export them in defiance of the one remaining restriction upon trade in the precious metals. All shillings in circulation were worn, clipped, and depreciated, and there was so much difficulty in keeping copper pence in circulation that the merchants were supplying tokens to satisfy the want of subsidiary coins. It is strange that when the merchants could use tokens it occurred to no one that the Government might solve its problems with respect to coinage in that manner, but then there was a lack of confidence in all governments and counterfeiters would also have interfered with a system of token coins. The demand for more coins, and for full-weight coins, resulted in the Act of 1666 for the encouragement of coining. It abolished all mint charges, and provided for the free coinage of both gold and silver bullion for anyone who brought them to the Mint. That Act caused England to shift to a gold standard, and confused all thinking about money in England for nearly two hundred years, and in the remainder of the world until the present; to it is directly attributable the controversy about the free coinage of silver which has disturbed the United States during nearly half of the time which has elapsed since 1876.

Although at the time the Act was passed there had been some coinage of gold, mostly for special purposes, it was too valuable for internal circulation, and there was little necessity for its coinage. Such gold coins as there were had a fluctuating price in silver shillings, and the direct connection of the Act with the coinage of gold was through the recently introduced "guinea." The origin of the guinea was in an Act passed a few years previous to 1666 to establish the African Company, the purpose of which was to trade with Africa. As the company brought in some gold, it was soon after its incorporation granted by the Government the privilege of having its gold coined at the Mint and stamped with its own insignia, or trade-mark, which was an elephant. At first that mark indicated that the gold in the coin had come from Guinea, and from that its name was derived. The guinea was supposed to be the equivalent of twenty silver shillings, and its coinage was at the rate of forty-four and one half from a pound of gold. That was adopted by the Act of 1666 as the rate of coinage for gold; and thus the official Mint price of gold was fixed at three pounds sterling, fourteen shillings, and two pence per ounce.

The Act retained the prevailing rate for silver, five shillings and two pence per ounce, two pence of which had been deducted by the government, but now all sixty-two were given to the one who brought the silver in for coinage. As an ounce of gold would bring nine hundred pence and an ounce of silver sixty-two, a Mint ratio of approximately 14.51 to one was established between the two metals. The open market ratio of exchange between the two metals was nearer to fifteen to one at the time, and but for one fact that would have prevented the coinage of any gold, as it was more valuable for exchange in commerce than for use as money at its Mint price. Guineas were received by the Government in payment of taxes at a premium which ranged from one shilling to as high as eight or nine, and they were also, as a necessary result of that, permitted to circulate at a premium. Consequently, there was a speculative element involved in taking gold to the Mint and receiving guineas which might be put into circulation at a time when they commanded a high premium, and they continued to circulate together with the silver shillings. This situation continued from 1666 until 1717, and in the meantime other important events occurred which must be considered before returning to the ultimate effects of the Free Coinage Act of 1666.

As the banking business was somewhat informally conducted by the goldsmiths, there was felt the need for an institution of a kind which would give it more stability, and a public bank established by the Government was advocated. Charles II resorted to an expedient which gave an important turn to the direction of affairs. It was in the nature of anticipating the collection of taxes, which was done by drawing orders on the Treasury for payment of money and assigning them to goldsmith bankers from whom he obtained loans. He also used them to some extent for the payment of expenses. As these orders were drawn and assigned they would be entered on a book in the Treasury for payment in sequence. The King naturally issued too many of such orders, and they went into default in 1672, remaining unpaid for about two years. Had Charles II or his ministers understood that the real opportunity offered by this practice was to create a means of paying taxes by issuing orders to the Treasury with no obligation whatsoever expressed on them, except that they be received in the payment of taxes at the number of pounds sterling stated, and had they been used for paying expenses, instead of borrowing money, the whole course of subsequent monetary history would have been entirely different. Whether that would have been for better or for worse no one can know. This unfortunate experience of Charles had one important result, however, which in view of the direction taken by monetary developments was probably for the better. Under Charles I some silver which had been brought to the Mint for coinage was seized by the King, and the memory of that "Stoppage of the Mint" combined with this "Stoppage of the Exchequer" by Charles II made everyone fearful of a bank subject to the control of a monarchy. Consequently, when the Bank of England was established, it was made a private institution — the effect of which will be considered later.

Probably the most important Act of Parliament during this period was the one in 1694, establishing the Bank of England. The subscribers to a fund of one million, two hundred thousand pounds sterling to be loaned to the Government were permitted to incorporate as a bank with the Government's indebtedness as its capital. A general banking business was authorized, and the Bank assumed the privilege of issuing bank notes, although it seems doubtful whether the Act was intended to have that effect.[4] Establishment of the Bank of England caused a great expansion of the banking business, as it became the fiscal agent of the Government, and could lend money at lower rates of interest than had previously been charged by the goldsmiths.

The use of paper money came in just as all the coin was being called in to the Mint to be brought up to standard by one of the recoinages which occurred periodically. Two more or less contemporary

[4] The sections of the Act of Parliament which authorized the establishment of the Bank of England are copied in the Appendix.

comments on this new practice of issuing paper money present opposite views: —

The Commons resolved to grant a supply, which should make up these deficiencies and give ample security for the punctual payment of tallies; the Act of 1697, not only enlarged the capital, and improved the status of the Bank of England, but restored the credit of the administration as well. Tallies, bank notes and Bank bills all began to circulate freely. Encouraged by his success, Montague proceeded to issue a large amount of paper currency in the form of Exchequer Bills, bearing interest; without some such money, it would have been physically impossible to collect the taxes required for the support of the war; but by these various expedients "Parliament laid a good Foundation for *Paper Money* to supply the Place of our Silver Coin; for so many Payments were at this time to be made into the *Exchequer,* that when the People had assurance given them that the *Exchequer* notes should be received back again in the payment of the King's Taxes, they were very well satisfied to take them, at first indeed at small Discount but not long after at an Equality. A great number of these Notes were only for Five or Ten Pounds which answered the necessity of Commerce among the Meaner People, for the Common Conveniences of Life. . . . These Bills passed as so many counters, which the People were satisfied to receive . . . and these State Counters so well supplied the want of Money, till New Coin was issued from the Mint, that Trade and Commerce were maintained, and Mutual Payments well enough made, to answer the Necessities of the Government and the People." [5]

The next one is almost typical of some complaints heard in the United States to-day: —

"The great Arrears of the Government like an Inundation, and all sorts of Paper creditt in Orders, Bills, Noats, Bonds, Assignments, etc., overflowed the Kingdom. All our wealth seem'd to consist in a little Gold and adulterated Silver, a world of wooden Scores and paper Sums. Never was there known before such vast debts owing for Excise and Customs, upon Bills and Bonds unsatisfyed. All sorts of Provisions grew to an extravagant Price, which was an additional hardship to day labourers and Artificers, besides their want of Mony and Credit. Upon the whole, wee had all the symptoms upon us of a Bankrupt sinking State and an undone people." [6]

About the time of this recoinage guineas had gone to a premium, their price being as high as thirty shillings, although they had been authorized on the supposition that they would be the equivalent of twenty shillings. The recoinage of the latter at full weight was instrumental in bringing down the

[5] Cunningham, "Growth of English Industry and Commerce", Vol. 2, p. 441, quoting from a contemporary source.

[6] *Ibid.*, Note 3, p. 440, quoting from Haynes, "Brief Memoirs relating to the Silver and Gold Coins of England", (1700).

price of guineas. At the same time, development of trade with the East and the export of large quantities of silver by the East India Company for use in that trade began to shift the open market ratio of exchange between silver and gold. Silver gained on gold. The Government desired a fixed price for the guinea, instead of having to accept it at varying prices, and after the guinea had fallen considerably in terms of the shilling a proclamation was issued fixing its price for acceptance by the Government at twenty-one shillings. That raised the official price of gold to three pounds sterling, seventeen shillings, and ten and a half pence per ounce — which made the Mint ratio between gold and silver approximately 15.07 to one. The same amount of gold was still coined into a guinea, but it was given a definite legal value by the action of the Government. As silver continued to appreciate in terms of gold, and the ratio of exchange between the two metals in the open market went to where less than fifteen parts of silver would exchange for one of gold, the Government did not change its proclaimed price for gold. The consequence was no one would take silver to the Mint, as it could be exchanged for gold, with which more money could be obtained. Thus the Free

Coinage Act of 1666 and a proclamation of the Government shifted England from a silver to a gold standard. It should be noticed that the origin of what is so inadequately described as "the Gold Standard", which, in one form or another, has prevailed in Great Britain from 1717 until the present, was directly connected with the taxing power.

Another consequence of the Act of 1666 was that it made impossible the keeping of silver coins in circulation if any gold was being coined. Since silver was undervalued at the Mint, any shilling coined was worth more as bullion than as money, and would be immediately melted down unless it was depreciated enough between the recoinage of 1698 and the shift to a gold standard in 1717 to remain in circulation. England struggled with this problem of the subsidiary coinage until it was solved in 1816 by making all silver coins tokens.

One good result of the Free Coinage Act was that it prepared the way for making the pound sterling the great instrument of modern commerce. Although the complete accomplishment of that was not reached until one hundred and eighty years after the Act of 1666, and that may seem to be a slow rate of progress, it is questionable whether the modern world is doing any better. The pound sterling in 1914 lost its ability to serve as the one great instrument of commerce among nations, and nearly twenty-one years have now elapsed without any satisfactory substitute for it being provided. The great effect of the shift to a gold standard in 1717 was to start the pound sterling on its way toward becoming an efficient Standard for all commerce wherever, within civilization, it was conducted. A comparatively large unit, the pound sterling tended to become the currency of merchants for the transaction of large business. The silver shilling tended to become the internal currency of England, and these two trends gradually caused a recognition in England of the distinction between money for internal use and a weight-account unit fixed with a metal for commerce among nations. Many writers who ignore the problem of creating a Standard for international commerce have criticized the Act of 1666 as an advantage obtained by the goldsmiths from an ignorant Parliament.[7] It is doubtful whether the gold-

---

[7] Del Mar's comments are typical of the kind: —

Was it to encourage the evasion of these imposts, and attract into the coffers of the London goldsmiths the metal upon which such imposts would have been levied, that Charles encouraged, rewarded, and distinguished the pirate Morgan, interdicted the coinage of silver at

smiths had such a great power to influence the Government, as they were not popular. The probability is that the desire of the merchants to return to the ancient use of contracts to deliver metal as a means of facilitating large commercial transactions was the motive which brought about the Act. So far as England is concerned, free coinage of the metals probably did as much good as harm, since in that country there has always been some understanding that there is a distinction between bullion and money; but it seems that the Act has misled the governments of other countries. The general result of free coinage has been to spread the impression that governments may engage in the creation of two kinds of money, one consisting of the coined metals, and the other of promises to pay such coins, with the relation between the two depending upon the convertibility of the second into the first. England drifted

Boston, Massachusetts, and surrendered to the London goldsmiths the royal prerogative of money? Whatever its object, it had far more mischievous results than were dreamed of at the time. . . .

The plain facts are these: two centuries ago the King of England plundered the goldsmiths in London of all their ready money. Either for the reasons already mentioned herein, or to compensate them for his father's injustice, his son substantially sold and surrendered to the goldsmiths the State prerogative of coinage.

— "The Science of Money", pp. 81, 83.

along this line for more than a century, and during that time there was very little progress in the development of her monetary laws.

The one important Act of Parliament, with relation to money, enacted in the entire eighteenth century was that of 1708, which prevented the establishment of any bank, other than the Bank of England or one by a partnership having less than seven members. That Act was generally accepted as meaning that no corporation could engage in banking. The intention was to give the Bank of England, as a corporation, a monopoly of the banking business, and it is to be noticed that the language of the provision was directed at the performance of contracts to pay money on demand. It did not merely prevent the circulation of certain kinds of evidence of the existence of such a contract.[8] A consequence of this Act was

[8] After reciting that the Act of 1696 for enlarging the capital stock of the Bank of England had forbidden the establishment of any "other bank, or any other corporation, society, fellowship, company, or constitution in the nature of a bank", and that "some corporations by colour of the charters to them granted, and other great numbers of persons", had presumed to borrow great sums of money, and "therewith contrary to the intent of the said act, do deal as a bank", the Act provided: —

From 29 Sept. 1708, during the continuance of the Governor and Company of the Bank of England, it shall not be lawful for any body politick or corporate whatsoever erected, or to be erected, other than

the growth of numerous small and independent country banks, which were subject to failures.

The encouragement in the use of bank notes attributable to the founding of the Bank of England caused a great development of the business of bank-

---

the said Governor and Company of the Bank of England, or for other persons, whatsoever united or to be united in covenants or partnership, exceeding the number of six persons, in that part of Great Britain called England, to borrow, owe, or take up any sum or sums of money on their bills or notes, payable at demand, or at any less time than six months from the borrowing thereof.

(6 Anne, C. 22.)

Contrast the legal accuracy and sufficiency to accomplish its purpose of this language with that of the Act of the Congress of the United States, 1866, 14 Statutes at Large, 146, Sec. 9: —

That every national banking association, State bank, or State banking association, shall pay a tax of ten per centum on the amount of notes of any person, State bank, or State banking association, used for circulation and paid out by them after the first day of August, 1866.

The English statute went to the heart of the matter by forbidding certain institutions to make any contract to pay money on demand: while the statute of the United States, the intended effect of which was the same, dealt with only one kind of evidence of the existence of such a contract, and failed to accomplish its purpose, which was to give national banks a monopoly of commercial banking.

Perhaps it should be said that the views expressed in this note are not in accord with what is said on the subject in the opinion of Chief Justice Tindal in the case of The Bank of England *v*. Anderson, 3 Bingham's New Cases, 589, at 635. The statute, 6 Anne C. 22, was there construed as forbidding the issuing of bank notes only, and not the making of contracts to pay money on demand, but that question was not involved in the decision of the case.

ing throughout England. While the goldsmiths became bankers in London some of the merchants got into the business of banking in other parts of England. The tendency to combine banking with merchandising began through the use of inland bills of exchange by the country merchants. They bought their goods in London and had to send coin there in payment. The large landowners sold their products in London, and in payment would receive bills on London. To dispose of these bills, in order that coin need not be transported, they would seek for persons who had payments to make in London, and would naturally go to the merchants as those who most frequently had to make payments there. First, the merchants began to deal in bills of exchange, and then to persuade those who had bills on London to leave the money with them at interest. They followed the practice of the goldsmiths in issuing receipts and notes for the money which they would obtain when the bills were paid in London. When a merchant who had accepted a bill for payment in London acquired from one who had sent agricultural products to London a bill also payable there he could offset one against the other and no transportation of coin was necessary.

When factories began to be established in certain counties of England the merchants in those sections who were in the habit of dealing in bills of exchange easily became bankers. A farmer who had received practically his whole income for a year from the sale of his products was glad to leave his money for safe-keeping with such a merchant. The small factory-owner was thus given a place to borrow, and also a means of discounting his bills on London for the sale of his products. As industry went on with great progress in England banking kept pace with it. It is said that in 1750 there were hardly twelve banks outside of London in all England, but by 1793 there were nearly four hundred.

Some parts of England remained agricultural and others went into manufacturing. The former became to a certain extent lenders of money and the latter borrowers. This was not done directly between the banks of the two sections, but through London as an intermediary. It became necessary for the country banks to have money on deposit in London, and they carried such accounts with the Bank of England. That bank then began to assume the duty of keeping banking reserves for the nation, and, although a privately owned institution, from that time

84

on it performed more and more functions public in their nature.

Although a system of checking accounts had not yet been developed, the private banks in London had a great many balances of indebtedness to strike between themselves. There were some orders for payment of money, drawn on banks, just as modern checks are; and of course there were many bills of exchange, both inland and foreign, to be settled between the banks. In the settlement of such accounts among themselves the banks naturally worked out an arrangement of paying balances only. This was done first by two banks directly offsetting against each other their respective promises to pay money. Then representatives of the various banks began to meet at stated intervals at a certain place, where the participating banks were regarded as an association, or a kind of separate entity known as the "clearinghouse." To the clearinghouse each bank paid the amount by which its responsibility for promises to pay exceeded such promises of the other banks held by it, or it received payment if the balance was the other way. The inconvenience of delivering money to settle these balances encouraged all banks to carry accounts with the Bank of Eng-

85

land, so that settlements could be made by those banks against which there was a balance drawing an order on the central bank, which was paid by charging its account and crediting another. This practice also gave greater importance to the Bank of England as a keeper of reserves for other banks, and it seems that there was a clearinghouse in existence as early as 1775.

The course of development tended to make Bank of England notes, silver shillings, and pence the internal money of England, the circulation of which was facilitated by the private banks engaging in the business of making contracts to pay money on demand. Their issuance of bank notes may be regarded as a part of the latter. There was the greatest freedom in the matter of issuing bank notes. The private banks were subject to no restrictions except those imposed by their own discretion, which was sometimes entirely inoperative as a check upon overexpansion of their notes. All restrictions upon the amount of Bank of England notes had also been removed, and that Bank was then tending to let the amount of gold it had on hand regulate the quantity of notes it had outstanding. The reversion in that respect to the gold reserve principle continued for nearly a century.

There was in 1774 an Act of Parliament which made more emphatic the shift from a silver to a gold standard by limiting the amount which could be legally tendered in silver coins to twenty-five pounds sterling. There was also a recoinage of both silver and gold at that time, but it was impossible to keep full-weight silver shillings in circulation. In a few years another recoinage was needed.

There were in 1790 few indications that England was within a half-century of making great and highly beneficial improvements in monetary legislation. In the meantime, due to the genius of Alexander Hamilton, progress went further in the United States; and it is necessary to consider what happened there before giving attention to the legislation in England which finally resulted in the successful creation of money for national use and at the same time a workable Standard for commerce among nations.

CHAPTER III

MONETARY PROGRESS IN THE UNITED STATES

IN considering the beginning of national monetary legislation in the United States it is necessary to keep in mind the conditions in that respect which prevailed in Colonial times. Some indications of the state of knowledge about finance in the world as a whole at that time are given by the fact that the British Parliament at no time attempted to provide for the colonies any kind of monetary system. Being left entirely to their own devices, and knowing that in other countries money was created in various ways by the action of governments, it was natural that the colonists should make some efforts to do the same thing for themselves. There was always a scarcity of the precious metals, and the balance of trade was generally against the colonies as a whole. English coins could not be taken from the country for use in the colonies, and they would not have remained had they been brought in. The disposition to assume the prerogative of coining money, as was tried in Massachusetts, was thwarted by the lack of precious metals. It did little good to try the issuance of any kind of notes promising to pay coined money, as not enough could be obtained to fulfill the promises. Therefore, the colonists resorted to the idea that paper money could be "based on" some valuable thing, such as wheat, tobacco, and even land. As the Spanish milled silver dollar began to circulate more in the colonies from the growth of trade with the possessions of that country, the use of notes promising to pay coins increased. The practice was carried to such extremes that Parliament forbade the colonies to issue any more paper money. Mere mention of the fact that all the evils of paper money, including that of making it legal tender, were felt in the colonies is sufficient for present purposes. Notwithstanding, the feeling that it was necessary and "useful" on occasion persisted, and there was always the cry for more money.

[When the Continental Congress was called upon to accomplish the almost impossible task of financing the Revolutionary War, resort to the issuance of some kind of paper money was inevitable. The story of how the expression "not worth a Continental" (note) came to be used in the United States, surviving to this day, needs no repetition here. There are, however, three points about that money which should be kept in mind.

First, the Continental Congress had no power to levy or collect taxes. It was entirely dependent upon grants of supplies from the states. If its notes had been secured by the existence of taxing power the total sum issued would not have been so appalling, and they would not have depreciated to such a great extent. They could not be used for the payment of taxes, and men naturally doubted that they ever would be paid, even after the Congress became the only governing body of an independent group of states.

Second, Congress itself recognized its lack of power to make the notes legal tender. That was done by the states at the request of Congress.

Third, the states as well as the Congress issued notes, and made their own notes legal tender. The consequence of that was that at the end of the War there were practically thirteen independent state currencies, all with violent individual fluctuations, and in addition a supposedly national currency almost without purchasing power.

From the first there was some tendency to establish a National Government, the beginning of that having been expressed by the Articles of Confederation adopted in 1778. The reluctance of the states to permit the acquisition of any power by the Congress is well illustrated by the second of those Articles.

Each State retains its sovereignty, freedom, and independence, and every power, jurisdiction, and right, which is not by this Confederation expressly delegated to the United States in Congress assembled.

Although the Articles of Confederation continued in effect until superseded by the Constitution, the taxing power was withheld from the Congress established by those Articles. Thus at the close of the War there was a large national debt without the power to collect taxes in order to pay it. The men who retained organic memories of Valley Forge, Saratoga, and Guilford Courthouse had intelligence enough to see that, in a world of land-stealing nations, the independence which had been achieved through their sacrifices would not long remain a reality unless they established a National Government of unified power. Of course, there were also motives arising out of economic conditions which deserve attention, but have probably been given too much.

The Constitution of the United States created a National Government which had not only the taxing power but other powers of equal importance. So far as this chapter goes into the subject of monetary legislation, it is sufficient to observe that in granting to the Congress power "to lay and collect Taxes" the Constitution gave to the National Government ample powers over both money and banking. It is unnecessary at this point to bring in other constitutional provisions which might have some bearing on the subject. One great reason for so much confusion in the United States about the constitutional power over money and banking has been the failure of economists, lawyers, and courts to understand that its source is to be found in the short clause conferring the taxing power. That includes the powers to coin money, to issue paper money, and to create and regulate all institutions which engage in the business of making contracts to pay money on demand.

Into a new government possessing such sovereign powers over money, jurisdiction over a wide territory potentially rich in natural resources, but sparsely populated, and with a staggering debt, Alexander Hamilton came as its first Secretary of the Treasury. His task was great, but so was the opportunity. Rarely, if ever, has there come to a statesman the chance to draft a set of monetary laws for a new nation without interference, or help, from another nation. Hamilton understood that he had to create and organize the institutions which could conduct the monetary process, and his success is largely attributable to the fact that he viewed the process as a whole.✳ ¹

The first step was to remove the obstacle placed by the default in the national debt, as to which "the necessities of the war, conspiring with inexperience in the subjects of finance, produced direct infractions, and . . . the subsequent period has been a continued scene of negative violation or non compliance." Congress had passed a resolution calling upon Hamilton to report on "a proper plan for the support of the public credit", and expressing its sentiment as being: —

That an adequate provision for the support of the public credit is a matter of high importance to the honor and prosperity of the United States.

93

In his report Hamilton said: "It is agreed, on all hands, that that part of the debt which has been contracted abroad, and is denominated the foreign debt, ought to be provided for according to the precise terms of the contracts relating to it." [1] The foreign debt, measured in the Spanish silver dollar, amounted to slightly less than twelve millions, including accrued interest; the "liquidated" domestic debt was a little more than forty millions, which included thirteen millions of interest past due; and the Continental notes were about two millions. In addition to that, the indebtedness of the individual states was in the aggregate around twenty-five millions. The questions were: on what terms the domestic debt should be refunded; whether the indebtedness of the states should be assumed by the National Government; and how the interest could be paid on the total, both foreign and domestic. Hamilton took the position that the debts of the states should be assumed, and outlined a taxation program which would enable the Government to pay the interest. Congress was finally persuaded on "assumption", the entire

---

[1] First Report on the Public Credit. "Papers", McKee ed., p. 10. In the beginning Hamilton quotes the Resolution of the House as above.

debt was funded — and then there was the question of how the taxes were to be paid.

The interest on the foreign debt was five hundred and forty-two thousand dollars a year, and on the domestic one million, seven hundred thousand, some of which also had to be sent abroad. As the money of the country consisted of foreign coin only, and it was doubtful at all times to what extent that could be retained in the internal circulation, Hamilton saw that it was absolutely necessary to create some means with which taxes could be paid. The Government might hope to collect the amount in coin necessary for foreign interest, but to try to do that for the total interest imposed a great burden.

Congress, in August, 1790, called upon Hamilton to make another report on further provision for establishing the public credit, his first report having been made in January of that year. This one he began by saying that he had "a conviction that a national bank is an institution of primary importance to the prosperous administration of the finances, and would be of the greatest utility in the operations connected with the support of the public credit." [2] In stressing the advantages of a bank he gave great

[2] Report on a National Bank, "Papers", McKee ed., p. 53.

95

prominence to the fact that "banks tend to facilitate the payment of taxes." When the observations made in his recommendation to Congress that a national bank be established are considered with his argument to President Washington that the Act of Congress creating the Bank was constitutional,[3] Hamilton's position appears as proposing to use the power "to designate or appoint the money or thing in which taxes are to be paid" as a means of creating money. It is to be remembered that there really was no money in the country at the time. What Hamilton proposed to do was to establish a bank and authorize it to issue bank notes, and to make those notes the means of paying taxes, which would also make them serve as a means of doing business within the country. That the principle was correct depends simply upon these facts: "the power to tax involves the power to destroy",[4] as well as to create, and, if the Government issues mere counters with which it says taxes must be paid, when the time for payment rolls around the possessor of land or chattels must turn in the proper number of those counters, or the hand

[3] "Papers", McKee ed., p. 99.

[4] Chief Justice Marshall in M'Culloch *v*. Maryland, 4 Wheaton 316, at 431.

of the law will seize what he possesses and deliver possession of it to one who will pay to the tax collector the required number of counters. Obviously, so long as a government issues no more of these counters than it collects in one year for its normal and prudent operating expenses, these counters will have a purchasing power as money. A new government, not in debt, might pay its first year's normal operating expenses in that manner, but not thereafter. The national indebtedness was a sufficient reason for designating a bank to issue these notes instead of having it done by the Government itself.

The bill which became the Act of Congress to establish the Bank of the United States was drafted by Hamilton as the charter of the bank.[5] Its capital was fixed at ten million dollars, one fourth of which was payable in specie — that is, in Spanish silver dollars — and the remainder in United States certificates of indebtedness. The Bank was authorized to do a general banking business, and the Government pledged itself not to create another bank during the life of its charter, which was limited to twenty years. It was provided that the Bank should

[5] Act of Feb. 25, 1791, 1 U. S. Statutes at Large, 191, which is copied in the Appendix.

not "directly or indirectly deal or trade in any thing, except bills of exchange, gold or silver bullion", but it was permitted to sell goods pledged for loans.

There was in the charter a prohibition against lending to the United States any sum greater than one hundred thousand dollars, or to any state a sum greater than fifty thousand dollars. Also the Bank was forbidden "to purchase any public debt what soever", but was permitted to sell any part of the certificates of public debt received on subscriptions to its stock.

The establishment of branches was authorized at the discretion of the Bank's directors, but the business to be done at branch banks was confined to deposits and discounts, which prevented them from issuing notes. In his recommendation of the creation of a national bank Hamilton had said: "There are at present three banks in the United States." [6] Also it is to be remembered that at the time the issuance of bank notes was considered an essential part of the business of a bank. Thus the provision in the charter authorizing branch banks indicates that Hamilton contemplated a national banking system spread over the country.

[6] "Papers", McKee ed., p. 73.

In its provisions concerning the note issue are the
most interesting features of the charter. The Bank
of England, from the organization of which Hamilton undoubtedly borrowed many features, had begun by having its note issue limited to the amount
of its capital. Then that limitation had been removed,
and none substituted for it. By 1791 the Bank of
England was beginning to evolve the metallic reserve theory of controlling its note issue, regarding
some proportion of gold to the amount of its notes
as giving the proper measure of what should be outstanding. That principle was incompatible with
Hamilton's idea of a reliance upon the taxing power
as a means of giving currency to a note issue. Under
the circumstances, it would have been very easy for
the ordinary statesman to have been misled by the
prevailing condition of the English laws, and, recog-
nizing the necessity for some limitation on note issues in a new and indebted nation, to have guessed
that the proper limitation was a metallic reserve requirement. Hamilton was wise enough, however, to
choose another method. The Bank was authorized
to issue notes, within the limitation that the indebtedness of the Bank should never exceed by more than
ten million dollars "the monies then actually de-

posited in the Bank for safe keeping." Those notes were made receivable in all payments to the Government, but were not made legal tender in private payments. It was required to deliver on demand coined money as called for by its notes, which in itself imposed a kind of metallic reserve requirement. This arrangement left a great deal to the discretion of the Bank. Perhaps some attention should be given to how it could work. If one took into the Bank coined money for a demand deposit he would receive its contract to repay it on demand, evidenced by either a bank note or a written memorandum of the credit. The contract, expressed either way, was a part of the indebtedness of the Bank. So was a contract to repay at a definite time a deposit of coin made to draw interest, in which case bank notes would not ever be issued to the depositor. In all three cases the effect of the limitation was the same as if bank notes had been issued to the depositor, as notes could not be issued to others, on the fact that the coin was there, without going into the limited amount of the ten millions. Thus the erection of an inflated superstructure of credit was prevented, and by the same means there was effective provision against any drastic deflation. So long as the Bank had on hand a sufficient quantity of coined money to meet demands it need not fear having to contract its note issue unduly. The guard against inflation, such as might have occurred on the gold reserve principle of issuing two to four paper dollars for each coined one obtained, was the best guard against deflation.

What really served as a check on the issue of notes was the demand for money as a means of paying taxes. In 1791 the revenues of the Government were four million, four hundred and nine thousand dollars; and ten years later that sum had grown to twelve million, nine hundred and thirty-five thousand.[7] Although the limit of ten million dollars on notes which might be issued without being any more than a substitute for coin held by the Bank might have been regarded as being too high at first, within less than a decade there was equally good reason for saying that it was too low. It is not to be overlooked that the states and their municipal subdivisions of government were also collecting taxes.

Thus the principle of a Fiduciary Issue of notes, that is to say, one which rests upon faith in the government of a nation, was introduced in the United

[7] "Financial History of the United States", Dewey, p. 110, Eleventh Edition.

States by Hamilton before it was adopted in England in its most complete aspects. That principle comes nearer to being the correct one for monetary legislation than any ever used in the preparation of that kind of laws. When it is properly correlated to the collection of taxes it becomes the one correct principle. The fact that there was a national debt payable in coined money of another nation prevented Hamilton from going all the way with the principle, as will be explained later.

One great defect in the charter of the Bank was that it was not given a complete monopoly of the business of making contracts to pay money on demand, which would have prevented any bank established by the states from issuing bank notes. That was impossible under the circumstances, however, as there was much argument about whether the Constitution conferred upon Congress the power to establish a bank. To demonstrate that there was such power required an argument from Hamilton to Washington, who had been advised by his Attorney General that the Act was unconstitutional and should be vetoed, and the paper submitted by Hamilton is one of the world's masterpieces of legal argument. Inclusion of such a provision would have enabled

Thomas Jefferson, who also contended that the Act was unconstitutional, to defeat the bill in Congress. The consequence of the omission of such a provision was that notes of banks chartered by the states would be paid into the Bank of the United States, and it would naturally present them for payment at once in order to obtain coined money for its own use. That caused great hostility against the Bank.

The Bank of the United States was an agency for the facilitation of commerce with other nations as well as that among the several states of the Union. Throughout its career of twenty years it was able to sell silver for its notes on demand, and, of course, it was always ready to buy both gold and silver when offered at the Mint price later established. There can be little doubt that the correct principle is that a bank, and not the Government, should deal in the precious metals for the purpose of making foreign exchanges. Hamilton has been criticized for making the Bank a private institution, not subject to complete control of the Government, although the Government was given a voice in its management by stockholdings. As matters are viewed to-day, the issue of notes, paper money, is a function of the Government. In those days, however, the privilege of issuing notes was considered an indispensable part of the business of banking; and that idea persisted in this country until it was proved to be erroneous by the results of legislation enacted after the Civil War. The Bank, according to that impression, could not exist without the privilege of issuing notes, and if the Bank was to do so it was not advisable for it to be done by the Government also. Furthermore, Government bills of credit, or notes, were in bad repute, and had Hamilton attempted to use them he would not have been regarded as establishing a sound financial system. Success, with resort to that practice, would have been very doubtful. Of the two evils, having a privately controlled central bank issuing notes, or having a government issuing notes and dealing in the precious metals, there can be no doubt about the latter being by far the greater one. Hamilton had to choose between the two, and he made the wiser choice.

In order to continue doing business, the Bank had to sell silver for its notes on demand, as to refuse would have been a violation of its charter. There was thus established in the United States at the beginning a free and open market in the precious metals. There were no restrictions imposed upon their export. The advantages to the country, at its birth as a nation, of this successful creation of a central bank to act as a public merchant in buying and selling the precious metals for the facilitation of foreign commerce can hardly be overestimated.

When the Bank of the United States went into operation, the country was in the anomalous position of having a national debt and bank notes without having any coined money of its own. There was general recognition of the fact that a Mint was needed, and Congress again requested Hamilton to make a report on that subject. His recommendations concerning the enactment of a coinage law and one for the establishment of a Mint are by no means as illuminating as his preceding reports. In this instance his work is to be judged by what he accomplished, with little reference to what he had to say about it. The Mint Act of 1792 [8] seems to have been of his authorship, although Jefferson had contributed the idea of using the decimal system in stating the denominations of money. That was expressed in the definition of the money of account, which was as follows: —

[8] Act of April 2, 1792, 1 U. S. Statutes at Large, 246.

The money of account of the United States shall be expressed in dollars or units, dimes or tenths, cents or hundredths, and milles or thousandths, a dime being the tenth part of a dollar, a cent the hundredth part of a dollar, a mille the thousandth part of a dollar, and [that] all accounts in the public offices and all proceedings in the courts of the United States shall be kept and had in conformity to this regulation.

The only coin which the Act authorized as the representative of the dollar was to be coined from 371.25 grains pure silver. Of the subsidiary coinage, dimes, quarters and half-dollars were made of silver, each containing its proportionate part of 371.25 grains of pure silver. One and five cent pieces were made of copper and nickel respectively.

Gold coins authorized were: eagles, "of the value of ten dollars or units, and to contain two hundred and forty-seven grains and four-eighths of a grain of pure . . . gold"; half-eagles, and quarter-eagles, each containing its proportionate number of grains of pure gold. The standard of the alloy used in the case of both metals was fixed at nine-tenths fine, and the legal price of gold is more frequently expressed in that standard.

What are commonly called the bimetallic features of a system of this kind must receive some attention.

It has been said that Jefferson was in favor of a silver standard; that Hamilton's idea was that gold should be used for large transactions and silver for small ones; and that in the discussion of the subject Hamilton said that the undervalued metal would not go into circulation, or would be driven out if already there.[9] The open market ratio of exchange between the two metals was approximately 15.2 of silver to one of gold, but probably for an accurate determination of that the most recent information from the London market was necessary. Although at that time such information when obtained was several weeks old, the market fluctuations were not so great as to bring the ratio of exchange between the two metals as low as fifteen to one, which was the Mint ratio selected by Hamilton — 24.75 grains of gold for a dollar and fifteen times that many, 371.25, of silver. In his report on the establishment of a Mint, Hamilton referred to "the legal proportion in the coins of Great Britain, which is as 1 to 15.2; but somewhat more than the actual or market proportion, which is not quite 1 to 15." If that statement of the market ratio of exchange between the metals

---

[9] William Graham Sumner, in his "Alexander Hamilton", criticizes Hamilton in connection with the Mint Act.

had been correct, the selection of a Mint proportion of 1 to 15 would have overvalued gold and established a gold standard, which it did not do. Also the statement that the legal proportion in Great Britain was 1 to 15.2 seems to have been incorrect. At another place in his report he said: "If gold be most convenient in large payments, silver is best adapted to the more minute and ordinary circulation."

Possibly the reason for overvaluing silver was directly connected with the necessity for dimes, quarters, and half-dollars in the circulation. Conditions prevailing at the time were different from those of to-day, and must be thoroughly understood in their bearing on this question. It has always been recognized that coins for small change cannot be made of gold, as its high price would make the coin far too little. If there had been selected a Mint ratio which placed and retained any gold coins in circulation, no silver coins could have remained in circulation, and Hamilton knew that. Also he could hardly have been completely ignorant of the difficulties about coined shillings which England was even then encountering. Perhaps Hamilton chose an overvaluation of silver as a substitute for making silver coins tokens, although his report does not so indicate. At the time, all nations were having trouble with subsidiary coins, and moreover all except England were on a silver standard of some kind. None had a sound system of coinage, and that was then of greater importance than it is now.

Whatever his reason for selecting the Mint ratio of fifteen to one between gold and silver, the Mint Act as drafted by Hamilton enabled the United States to begin by maintaining an adequate circulation of small coins, and it was the only nation in the world to do so at the time. The presence of small coins in the circulation practically prevents the issue of small bank notes, and the absence of the former almost compels the presence of the latter. Further attention to this subject will be given when the consequences of subsequent monetary legislation in the United States are considered in the fifth chapter.

With the financial system established by Hamilton the United States began its march along the road to prosperity. There is no occasion to exaggerate by saying that Hamilton created that prosperity; but he certainly created the only kind of institutions which at that time would have aided in its achievement, instead of being hindrances, as institutions of the kind which we have had since his were superseded would have been. It is to be noticed that a serious depression of the so-called "secondary postwar" type did not come after the Revolutionary War, and that is the only time in the history of the United States that one of that kind did not come within approximately a quarter of a century after a great war.

There was no public credit, Hamilton created it. There was no circulating medium, no financial machinery: he supplied them. Business was languishing, and business revived.[10]

Although these comments of Henry Cabot Lodge on the work of Hamilton are high praise, they do not adequately describe what he did. That was to provide for the circulation of money at the same time provision was made for commerce with other nations. In view of the state of knowledge at that time, when no other nation had even a comparable system, the achievement should be given recognition as the greatest work ever performed by one statesman.

[10] "Alexander Hamilton", Lodge, American Statesmen Series, p. 132.

CHAPTER IV

GREAT BRITAIN CREATES A STANDARD OF INTERNATIONAL TRADE

THE pre-eminent position of Great Britain as a world power was not reached until after the Napoleonic Wars. As was the condition in the United States approximately one hundred years later, the monetary laws of Great Britain in 1815 were not suitable for performing successfully the rôle of leading nation. In many respects the defects in both systems at the respective times were similar, the excellent organization established by Hamilton in the United States having been abandoned for nearly a century in 1919. Experience taught some hard lessons to the members of the British Parliament, and they gradually learned to enact laws which provided remedies.

To maintain its own armies and navies, and to aid in the maintenance of allied armies in the wars against Napoleon, severely taxed the British treasury. Pitt, as Prime Minister, forced the Bank of England to make loan after loan to the Government in amounts which were generally considered to be excessive.[1] The result was that the note issue was greatly expanded, and the pound sterling began to lose its ability to buy gold. Finally, the Bank became unable to make deliveries of gold in exchange for its notes, and the requirement that it do so was suspended by Act of Parliament. During this period of "Bank Restriction", as it was called, the greatest extent to which Bank of England notes depreciated was twenty-two pounds and eighteen shillings on a hundred, which was in 1813.[2] Prior to that time, however, the high price of gold bullion had attracted general attention, and Parliament had appointed a Committee to investigate and report.

The report of that Committee, known as the Bullion Committee, was made in 1810. The important part of the report, for present purposes, was its conclusion that the high price of gold bullion in Bank of England notes was caused by the fact that the amount of notes issued was excessive. Parliament debated the report, and rejected its conclusions. Shortly after termination of the wars, however, the

---

[1] "History of the Bank of England", Andréadès, p. 174.

[2] "The Pound Sterling", Feaveryear, p. 194, to which a general reference is made for factual support of the first part of this chapter.

subject was again considered and then Parliament
reversed its decision. The report of the Bullion Committee undoubtedly served greatly in preparing the
way for important features of the Bank Charter
of 1844, as well as the amending Act of 1833.[3] Ac-

[3] The report of the Bullion Committee is analyzed in Chap. V
of Andréadès' "History of the Bank of England", and extensively
commented on in William Graham Sumner's "History of American Currency." On p. 221 of the former, the most important
points covered in the report are stated as follows: —

1. Whether the notes were depreciated, or whether, on the contrary, the price of gold had actually risen.
2. Whether the increase in the issue had any influence upon the
rate of the exchanges.
3. What effect a restriction of the issues would have on the price
of gold and the rate of the exchanges.
4. What policy ought to be followed with regard to the regulation
of the issues.

The answers of the Committee to the first three questions were
as follows: 1. That the notes were depreciated and the price of
gold had not risen. 2. That the increase in the note issue was responsible for the rates of international exchange being against
England. 3. That a restriction of the note issue would restore to
par both the ability of the notes to buy gold, and the rate of foreign exchange.

One witness who contended that the notes had not depreciated replied to an embarrassing question by saying: "I do not
conceive gold to be a fairer standard for Bank of England notes
than indigo or broadcloth." (*Ibid.*, p. 223.) Was this remark a
forerunner of the "commodity dollar" theory?

On the whole, the work of this Committee was excellent. It
may be criticized for failing to recognize foreign trade as barter,
and for its emphasis on money as a "measure of value."

cording to the law of coinage the price of gold in 1816 was three pounds, seventeen shillings, ten and a half pence per ounce — that is to say, that was the ratio at which guineas might have been coined had any gold been going to the Mint then; but actually gold was selling well above four pounds sterling per ounce.

After the Napoleonic Wars the Bank of England continued to be unable to deliver gold for its notes at par, and the subsidiary silver coinage of the country was in very bad condition. A great debate about the high price of gold had been conducted between the supporters of the report of the Bullion Committee, who contended that excess in the issue of notes by the Bank was the cause, and those who attributed the great rise in the value of gold to other conditions. There seems to have been little general demand in the year 1816 for an increase of the Mint price of gold to make it correspond to the open-market pound sterling price. The prevailing opinion was that the old price of gold, three pounds, seventeen shillings, and ten and a half pence, should and would be restored. At the time, however, there was probably more determination than comprehension. A committee of the Privy Council originally appointed in 1798 had from that time on been studying currency questions, and they made a report at this time. The recommendations of that committee were for a reform of the silver coinage and a new gold coin.

As to silver, shillings were to be coined from that metal at the rate of sixty-six instead of sixty-two per ounce. They recommended further, however, that the Mint should still purchase silver at the rate of sixty-two pence per ounce, but fortunately that was not adopted. With the price of gold at par in pound sterling notes of the Bank of England, enactment of legislation overvaluing silver made the silver shillings tokens in nature to some extent, as their legal value was then above their bullion value. That prevented them from being melted for silver bullion to sell, and enabled them to remain in circulation. Another feature of the Act of 1816 was that silver shillings were limited, as legal tender, to forty shillings.

The Act did not require that the Mint be opened to all comers for the purchase of silver at the rate of sixty-two shillings per ounce, but left that subject to proclamation. Such a proclamation was not issued; and from that time on the Government bought, at open-market prices, all silver required for sub-sidiary coins, and they remained in circulation. Thus there was corrected a mistake made more than one hundred years previously, by the combination of the Free Coinage Act of 1866 and, a few years later, the fixing of the guinea at twenty-one shillings.

The Act of Parliament in 1816 also displaced the guinea with the sovereign. A twenty-shilling gold coin was recommended by the committee upon whose report Parliament based its action. It is to be noted that the Mint price of gold was left unchanged, the only difference made being that the one gold coin in circulation was made the equivalent of the pound sterling. There was no change in the standard, which had been a gold standard for nearly one hundred years, although the pound sterling was tied to gold somewhat more firmly, and probably more by design, than had hitherto been the case. Until that time, if the Act of 1774 limiting the legal-tender value of silver is ignored, it had been, theoretically, possible for England to be shifted back to a silver standard by a drop in the open-market ratio of exchange be-tween silver and gold.

In view of the unhappy experiences in the efforts to keep full-weight silver shillings in circulation, what happened to the new sovereigns as soon as they were coined is interesting. The price of gold in pounds sterling fell temporarily in 1816, and many sovereigns were coined. But after a year or more the price of gold rose again to above the Mint price, and then all the new sovereigns went abroad. It had been perfectly demonstrated in the case of the subsidiary coins of silver that the value and quantity of metal should not be allowed to control the circulation, and sometimes cause a want of circulation of those coins. Although shillings were not used for large payments, their presence was absolutely necessary for small ones. They were taken from complete subjection to metal. That in itself showed that the internal circulation of money is on a principle entirely different from the circulation of the precious metals in commerce among nations. The problem was to provide adequately for the internal circulation of money so as to ensure at the same time the ability of that money to buy gold at a fixed price for use in foreign commerce. Part of that problem, so far as it related to the subsidiary currency, was solved by the Act of 1816; but as to gold, the solution of the problem was postponed until the Bank Charter Act in 1844.

With Bank of England notes unable to buy gold at par, the legislation of 1816 did not have any effect toward returning the country to a fixed instead of fluctuating gold standard. Another committee of Parliament, that of 1819, went to work. They were convinced that there must be a return to a fixed-price gold standard along the lines laid out by the Act of 1816. An increase in the price of gold was hardly contemplated, and it was necessary to restore the ability of the Bank of England to sell gold for its own notes at the price of three pounds, seventeen shillings, ten and a half pence per ounce. Gold was then four pounds, one shilling per ounce.

The principles announced by the Bullion Committee were adopted in full by the Committee of 1819. Too many Bank of England notes had caused the rise in the price of gold. Therefore the note issue had to be contracted. In effect the report of the Committee of 1819, and the action of Parliament upon that report, made the Bank of England the manager of the currency of the country. The situation was that the depreciated Bank Notes were the main part of the currency of the country, and Parliament, doing no more than providing for payment of some of the Government's indebtedness to the Bank, imposed upon it the task of bringing the notes to par. The Bank's directors protested that it was a private institution, and should not be charged with such a burdensome duty. Parliament, however, adhered to the policy.

Decreasing the note issue of the Bank of England was carried to extremes, and too much deflation resulted. That, however, is of little interest here, except to support the contention that the Act of 1816 did not establish a workable standard.

In the meantime, private bankers were allowed to continue their note issues. They were not regulated, and those banks, being many small independent units, frequently failed. Also, the note issues of the Bank of England were not subject to Government control in amount. The Bank was allowed to use its own judgment in the expansion and contraction of notes, without any statutory principle being applicable. There was not complete legislative recognition of the distinctions between the internal circulation of money and the international circulation of the precious metals, although making the shilling a token coin had been a step in that direction. The Bank was supposed to observe the rates of foreign exchange, and govern its note issue and loans according to that. Two great principles later supplied were lacking.

The legislation of 1819 also repealed the restrictions against melting the coins of either metal into bullion and exporting it. If gold coins were to be placed in circulation that action was necessary for the existence of a free and open market in gold. It was at this time that Ricardo made his proposal that there be no more coinage of gold, and that the Bank be required to buy and sell bullion only. In his work on "Political Economy", discussing foreign trade, Ricardo said that the precious metals tended to be distributed among the nations on a barter basis.

Until some time after the report of the Committee of 1819, the Bank of England had competed with the bill brokers and other banks in the discount market. After the Napoleonic Wars the availability of large amounts of Government bonds and large-scale industrial developments gave it other opportunities for investment. Then the management of the Bank evolved the idea that the Bank's rate of discount should always be above the market rate, so that ordinarily bills would not be brought there for discount. The Bank would constitute a reserve for the bill brokers, but would not contribute to overexpansion of credit by competing in the market. It was prevented from effectively carrying out this policy by a law forbidding the charging of interest at a rate higher than five per cent. The Bank Charter Act of 1833 repealed this law, so far as bills and notes with maturity not longer than three months from date were concerned. That was another great step toward freedom of contract. Thereafter, the Bank could exercise some control over the discount market by lowering and raising its discount rate.

Another improvement made by the Bank Charter Act of 1833 was in making notes of the Bank of England legal tender except by the Bank itself for amounts greater than five pounds, so long as it was able to sell gold for its notes at par. The advantage of this was in the fact that a run on a country bank could be met by paying out these notes, without the necessity of drawing on the gold reserves in London. This was a step toward making the gold of the Bank of England free for sale in commerce with other nations. Here was the second recognition of the distinction between the internal circulation of money and the external circulation of metal, the first having occurred when the subsidiary silver coins were given the nature of tokens.

The Act of 1833 also permitted joint-stock companies to operate in London and its hitherto forbidden radius of sixty-five miles, provided they did not issue bank notes. This made possible the development of the great joint-stock banks, as they could now have their headquarters in London and branches in the country. The banking system of the nation was greatly strengthened.

As the joint-stock banks established in London could not issue bank notes, their development tended toward the modern system of checking accounts. For a long time it had been possible to draw orders on a bank to pay money to the person to whom the order was given, and although previously little used, this kind of order quickly turned into the check used to-day. It is important to notice the real nature of the business of banking at this stage.

Under this system, the one who brought money to a bank exchanged his money for a contract of the bank to pay out, as directed by the person with whom the contract was made, an equivalent amount of money. It was not a deposit of money, although that term continued to be used, but an exchange of money for a contract. The depositor was a creditor of the bank, which was his debtor.

A change was also made in the method of a bank making loans. Instead of lending its credit to a customer by issuing bank notes to him, the bank made a contract with the borrower that it would pay out as he directed, by means of checks, a certain sum of money. The borrower gave the bank his promise to pay the same sum of money to the bank on a certain day. In other words, the obligation of the bank was to pay on demand, and the obligation of the borrower was to repay the bank at a certain time, usually within three months from the date of the transaction.

When a bank issued notes it loaned its credit to its customer, but when a checking account was substituted for bank notes the bank ceased to lend its credit, except in some special instances. The person to whom the customer paid the bank notes probably had no relations of any kind with the bank, and unless the bank was well known might not desire to use or trust its credit any longer than it would take to present the notes for payment. Therefore the bank had to be better prepared to make payments while it was issuing bank notes, that is, it had to keep on hand more legal tender money in proportion to notes than to deposits. The probability of all the notes issued to one person being presented for payment at once was much greater than the probability of a total sum deposited being drawn out at once. Also the banker's ability to make payment by charging the account of one customer at the same time he credited the account of another was greatly increased by this change in the nature of the business. The consequence was a great expansion in the making of contracts to pay money on demand by banks, which is commonly called credit expansion, and may easily go into inflation.

Thus the Bank of England really had two kinds of reserves to keep, one for internal use, and the other for commerce with other nations. The first could be held in money good internally only, or in its own notes, since they had been made legal tender by the private banks, but the second had to be kept in gold. Here were the great defects of the Act of 1816 and the Bank Charter Act of 1833, which were the failures of both to allow for the fact that the principles applicable to the maintenance of the two reserves were essentially different.

No monopoly of note issuing had been conferred

upon the Bank of England up to this time. The country banks outside of the sixty-five mile radius from London were still permitted to issue bank notes. Thus they had not lost all their power to create an overexpansion of bank credit. In fact, that power had been increased in one way, which was by permitting them to make legal tenders in Bank of England notes to an extent limited as above noted.

The Bank of England considered that it was in almost perfect condition so long as its promises to deliver both gold coin and bullion did not exceed by more than three times the amount of gold it had on hand. These promises were made both in bank notes and contracts with depositors. There was no limit imposed by law upon the expansion of either bank notes or deposits, the Bank's judgment as to the proper management in this respect being unhampered. Consequently, as gold entered in larger quantities the Bank was naturally induced to expand the use of its credit, in both issues of notes and the granting of discounts. This in turn permitted expansion by the joint-stock and country banks. The credit structure as a whole could be regarded as a kind of inverted pyramid, the "base" being of gold, the first stage of the superstructure Bank of

England notes and deposits, the second stage notes of the country banks, and the third stage all the promises of the banks, other than the Bank of England, to pay money on demand. Just as this superstructure could be built up by the acquisition of gold expanding the "base", so was its removal in part, or tearing down, made inevitable by the loss of gold and the contraction of the "base." Neither the Bank of England nor the Government of Great Britain understood by 1833 that gold can make "unsound" money just as readily as paper. The dangerous nature of inflationary expansion of credit on a "gold base" had not been comprehended at that time.

Leading up to the Bank Charter Act of 1844 was a succession of expansions and contractions of the credit superstructure. For a while after 1833 the gold stocks of the Bank of England rose, and it expanded both notes and discounts. Then the Bank began to lose gold, and was forced to contract both. After this crisis was met, the gold stock of the Bank began to rise again; and in 1837 it reached ten and a half million pounds sterling, a comparatively high figure for those days. Again, overexpansion resulted; and there was another forced contraction when the loss of gold brought the Bank's stock down to two and one-half millions. Parliament decided that conditions required another committee. It should be added here that the Bank had not always adhered to its stated policy of limiting notes and discounts to three times the amount of gold on hand. The practical impossibility of that shows that the principle was not correct.

As to the principles upon which the monetary institutions of Great Britain operated from 1819 until 1844, it is to be observed that one was that of the gold reserve, — although there was no statutory requirement in that respect, — and the other, somewhat subject to the first, was that of a "managed currency." The directors of the Bank of England had developed the first principle mostly on their own initiative, and the second, to some extent, had been established by Act of Parliament. Experience convinced the statesmen of the country that neither principle would work, and further legislative changes began to be discussed by two schools of thought. One was called the Currency School, and was at the time, as it has been since then, charged with giving undue emphasis to bank notes. The other was called the Banking School, and contended that what they called

"Deposit Currency" was the more important. Evidently the former — who prevailed, fortunately — understood that the business of banking, so far as institutions other than a central bank are concerned, consists of making contracts to pay money; that the business of a central bank consists of the making of such contracts for reserve purposes and dealing in gold for the aid of foreign trade; and that, in a nation of the wealth and power of Great Britain at the time, money for internal commerce and industry was one thing and gold for foreign trade another. These principles do not ever seem to be comprehended by anyone who speaks of "deposit currency", and thus confuses a check — which is not more than evidence of the existence of a contract to pay money — with the money which the check says a bank has promised to pay. By that time a Bank of England note was not a promise to pay money, but was money itself, with which gold could be bought and any other bank's contract to pay money discharged. Sir Robert Peel was the leader of the Currency School, which prepared the great Bank Charter Act of 1844.

That Act divided the Bank of England into two departments, one the Issue Department, the function of which was to issue bank notes, and the other the Banking Department, which was to do all the other business of the Bank. Then it required that the Bank set apart to the Issue Department securities and some bullion valued at fourteen million pounds sterling, of which the public debt held by the Bank should be a part, and that the Issue Department then deliver to the Banking Department fourteen million pounds in Bank of England notes. This fourteen million pounds was appropriately called the Fiduciary Issue, as it was not "based on" gold, but depended upon the stability, power, integrity, and intelligence of the British Government. In other words, it rested upon faith in the Government. Its existence was not made dependent upon the possession of gold.

The Act then provided: —

From and after such transfer and appropriation to the said Issue Department as aforesaid it shall not be lawful for the said Governor and Company to issue Bank of England notes, either into the Banking Department of the Bank of England, or to any Persons or Person whatsoever, save in exchange for other Bank of England notes, or for Gold Coin or for Gold or Silver Bullion received or purchased for the said Issue Department under the Provisions of this Act.

The amount of silver that the Bank could buy with the issuance of notes was limited, and silver was not ever carried in the reserves of the Bank to any great extent.

Another provision was that: —

All Persons shall be entitled to demand from the Issue Department of the Bank of England Bank of England Notes in exchange for Gold Bullion, at the rate of Three Pounds Seventeen Shillings and Nine Pence per ounce of Standard Gold.[4]

There was, in previous laws relating to the Bank, a requirement that it sell gold for its notes at the price of three pounds, seventeen shillings, and ten and one-half pence per ounce. In brief, the effect of the Act was to make the Bank a public merchant in gold charged by law with the duty of selling gold and buying it for the benefit of the country's commerce with other nations. There was a clear, and successful, recognition of the distinction between the internal circulation of currency and the circulation of gold in commerce among nations. As the entire note issue of the Bank at the time was less than twenty million pounds sterling, the Fiduciary Issue of fourteen millions, in conjunction with the

[4] 7 and 8 Vict. C. 32.

subsidiary silver coinage, practically created an internal currency which was free from the control of gold. The business of the banks, other than the Bank of England, was not in making contracts to deliver gold, but contracts to pay money on demand. The Act of 1844 created money which was good and sufficient for the purpose. By abandoning the fallacious gold-reserve principle, it freed the money of the nation from the chance of becoming greatly overexpanded on account of the natural impulse to erect too great a superstructure on a broadening gold base. At the same time it freed it from the chance of being suddenly and disastrously contracted too much on account of a loss of gold. Thus the Fiduciary Issue served as a guard against inflation, which made it the best protection against deflation. The best proof of this is that from 1844 to 1914 there was practically no fear at any time that the Bank of England would be unable to sell gold for its notes at par. The Fiduciary Issue also served to free gold from the claims of support for internal currency so that it might be available for the purposes of foreign trade. There was recognition of the fact that commerce with other nations is barter in which gold is used as a commodity. It is to be noticed that after a trial of twenty-seven years the "managed currency" theory was also abandoned.

The Act of 1844 also provided for the gradual elimination of the issue of bank notes by banks other than the Bank of England. No newly established bank was to be permitted to issue notes, and any private bank exercising the privilege was to lose it when converted into, or absorbed by, a joint-stock bank. Provision was made for the increase of the Fiduciary Issue by giving to the Bank of England authority to add to its notes of that kind two thirds of the amount retired by any private bank ceasing to exercise the privilege. The Fiduciary Issue was finally increased, by this method, to nineteen million, seven hundred fifty thousand pounds, when, in 1923, the last private bank ceased to issue notes.

The Bank Charter Act of 1844 was the final preparation of the monetary institutions of Great Britain for the rôle the nation was to play so successfully, until 1914, as the administrator of the Standard of international commerce. It established, and ensured the maintenance of, a free and open gold market in London, which was the only one that the world had during that period. Finally, it was possible freely to make and perform contracts for the delivery of gold.

There was, however, one remaining restriction upon the markets of Great Britain. The nation did not afford a free and open market for goods. That came in 1846, with the repeal of the Corn Laws and other forms of import restrictions. Thus when freedom of contract in buying and selling goods was permitted by legislation there was in London a free and open market for both gold and goods. Then the monetary process could be carried on to the highest degree of success. The pound sterling became a monetary unit, which would always buy gold at par and could always be bought with goods, both without legal restrictions. A Standard of International Trade was finally created when the monetary unit upon which the Standard had to be founded became subject to acquisition by the free delivery of goods in the markets of the nation which created the Standard. On such terms only may there be a Standard of payments in commerce among nations. That was demonstrated in Great Britain from 1815 to 1846, and has been in the course of demonstration in the United States ever since November 11, 1918.

Great Britain did more than establish and administer a Standard of International Trade during the period mentioned above. She recognized and performed the duties of leading nation, and so directed international affairs that the monetary process could be carried on all over the world in comparative peace and freedom. Anyone who reflects upon the history of world affairs for the seventy years preceding 1914 may well doubt that, had Great Britain retained her pre-eminent position after 1918, there would be so many probabilities of wars to-day.

There follows an attempt to state the principles of the monetary process to be learned from the experience and laws of Great Britain on the subject. It must be emphasized, however, that these principles are stated as being applicable to the most powerful nation only, and it is assumed that such a nation has a government of great stability, power, intelligence, and integrity. Those principles are: —

I. There must be a free and open market for gold, except for one restriction, which is a fixed price.

II. There must also be a free and open market for goods.

III. The money of the nation must always be able to buy gold at a fixed price, but must be neither dependent upon gold for its existence, nor subject to the control of gold so as to permit either great expansion or contraction.

IV. There must be a Central Bank to act as a public merchant in buying and selling gold, for all comers, at a fixed price, and this branch of its business must be run on the principle of maintaining a supply of gold adequate to meet demands but not excessive. The Central Bank must also serve as a reserve bank for all other banks.

V. There must be a good system of banks for checking accounts, able to perform without question all their contracts to pay money on demand.

It is necessary to make some comments on these principles as they apply to the use of gold for monetary purposes in nations inferior to the leading one, and in commerce among nations. The immediate means by which the internal monetary process of Great Britain was carried on were largely created by law. These were the Fiduciary Issue of notes, token coins, and checks. Accomplishment of this was utterly impossible for any other nation in the world. Their governments had not sufficient power or stability, rarely the intelligence, and sometimes not the integrity, to dare take the position that they would create money by law. Mention of a few well-known facts will be sufficient to show this.

In less than a century from 1789, France was governed by three monarchies, if the change in 1830 is counted, three republics, and two empires. Obviously stability was lacking, and the Franco-Prussian War showed that power was lacking. The French people have consistently refused to be taxed enough to support their government properly, and no nation which habitually fails to balance its budget can hope to create money successfully in any way except by coining the precious metals. Also France hardly knew banks which carried checking accounts, and the people were inclined to hoard gold.

Germany and Italy were not nations in 1844, but after they became nations no one knew exactly what in the way of stability might be expected from their governments. Russia and Austria-Hungary were in a condition little better. The facts that Germany within little more than a half-century from its birth as a nation abolished its money entirely by a grand inflation, that Italy within about the same length of time devalued her currency by three quarters, and France hers by four fifths, and that the then existing currencies of Russia and Austria-Hungary have been completely obliterated, are all highly significant.

The United States had foolishly abandoned the financial system established by Alexander Hamilton; and its people, at that time, would tolerate neither a national bank nor a national currency.

Consequently, all these nations had to have either gold or silver if they were to have any kind of money worthy of the name. They were practically all on a standard of the kind ordinarily called bimetallic — that is, they shifted to either metal as it fell in the open-market ratio of exchange with the other. The successful working of what they mistakenly called "the gold standard" for Great Britain aroused their envy. As they grew stronger, there became more urgent the desire to compete in international trade; but they were handicapped by the fact that they were not "on" the prevailing standard. Neither alone nor in combination could they establish a rival standard. Therefore, all other nations of commercial importance were practically compelled to try to follow the example of Great Britain as best they could. They went "on the gold standard" not from choice, but from the necessities of commerce. Either their governments misunderstood what they were attempting to do, or dared not represent themselves as having the necessary qualities to enact and live up to the kind of laws which should have been adopted.[5]

Once "on the gold standard" the ability of these other nations to stay there was largely at the mercy of Great Britain. Should they be forced to abandon the standard adopted, without regard to what kind of standard it was, such a revelation of weakness would have been destructive of confidence and disturbing to business. The legal effect of making all contracts dischargeable by delivery of gold was tremendous, and especially so in view of the fact that none of the secondary nations had currencies supportable internally without the use of gold. Their very weakness made the possession of comparatively large stocks of gold absolutely necessary. In other words, London had the power to take the gold from

[5] England, once possessed of a gold standard, is the model Power because she is the strongest. It was because the other Powers wished to enter into stable inter-valutary relations with her that . . . the gold standard spread.
— Knapp, "The State Theory of Money", p. 278.

It was not the gold standard *per se* that spread after 1871, but the English monetary system, which was the gold standard merely as it were by accident.
— *Ibid.*, p. 279.

them, but if that power had been used Great Britain would have lost many valuable customers. The result was that the Bank of England had to take the risk of administering the Standard of International Trade with a stock of gold that was always smaller, in proportion to power and national wealth, than that of almost any of the other nations, and frequently actually smaller. The Bank of England performed the function of keeping gold distributed so that other nations could support their currencies.

Anyone who examines typical statements of the Bank of England's condition from 1844 to 1914 will be impressed with the fact that it did not hoard gold. It is significant that a Committee of Parliament appointed to investigate the causes of a financial crisis in 1857 reported that one cause had been that too much gold had come in, and that inflation had resulted. A good illustration of the Bank's policy is to be found in its action during the Panic of 1907 in the United States. At that time the Bank of England had on hand only nineteen million pounds sterling worth of gold. New York was begging for gold, but no one of the other nations which had most of the gold would send a dollar's worth to the United States. The Bank of England forced those nations to send gold worth twenty-five million pounds sterling to London, then sent it to New York, and thereby helped to terminate the Panic. At the end of the year 1913, according to reliable [6] estimates, the total amount of monetary gold in Great Britain was, measured by dollars, eight hundred and thirty millions, of which the Bank of England held one hundred and sixty-five millions. This total was barely ten per cent. of the world's stock. At the time, France, Germany, and Russia each held an appreciably greater percentage, and the United States had twenty-three per cent. Obviously Great Britain's portion was

[6] Withers, "The Meaning of Money", pp. 100, 292. In Andréadès' "History of The Bank of England", p. 267, there is the following comment on the export of gold at another time: —

During this time the Bank of England had been acting in a manner very far from prudent. Seeing that gold came in plentifully, it reduced its rate of discount from 5 to 4 per cent., and in November, 1838, even to 3½ per cent. Consequently, at this latter date, at the very moment when the collapse of the Bank of Belgium gave clear warning of the imminence of a serious drain, the Bank rate was lower than the market rate. By way of meeting the danger, and not content with increasing its discounts when it was evident that everyone was exporting gold to America, the Bank thought fit — in the face of an unfavourable exchange — to send a million to America on its own account! Of all acts of mis-management in the whole history of the Bank, says Macleod, this is probably the most astounding.

In view of conditions prevailing in the United States in 1838, one may well consider whether the action of the Bank was the performance of an international duty in a crisis. Perhaps the only just criticism is that there was more courage than caution.

neither as great as her wealth would have indicated nor as great as her power to command would have brought in had she chosen to exercise it.

Only the excellence of the laws relating to the monetary process in Great Britain permitted the Bank of England to assume the risk of administering the Standard of International Trade in any such manner. Although it was successfully accomplished, at the same time it was risky. The Acts of 1833 and 1844 had permitted the joint-stock banks to grow and improve so that their contracts to pay money on demand were good substitutes for the use of gold internally. The Fiduciary Issue went far toward supplying that money without the use of gold. Had the Bank been compelled by law to possess great hoards of gold for use internally to support the currency of the nation, it could not have administered the international Standard. It was also aided materially by repeal of the law fixing a maximum interest rate. That enabled it practically to bring gold in when needed by raising the amount of rent offered for it. Although, when gold was thus brought in by raising the discount rate, title passed through a sale of the gold to the Bank for a credit on its books, the sellers knew that they could repurchase a similar quantity of gold whenever it became more profitable to have the gold for use elsewhere. The effect was that gold could be rented to the Bank of England with return on demand certain.

It was not gold alone, however, which made the British administration of the Standard of International Trade such a great force for world prosperity. In fact, the importance of gold has probably been greatly exaggerated in this chapter. There was undoubtedly a great advantage in having gold serve as a kind of common denominator for the making of contracts in commerce among nations; but of greater importance was the fact that the power of the leading nation was exerted to the end that men all over the world might make contracts to deliver gold with the assurance that those contracts could be discharged through the delivery of goods.

The Standard of International Trade was not a weight of gold, and is not adequately described as being either "the Gold Standard" or a gold standard. All other nations had to adjust their monetary systems so that their legal price for gold was in accord with that established by Great Britain. The legal arrangements according to which the monetary institutions of Great Britain operated, with respect to both that country's internal commerce and industry and commerce among nations, tended to prevent variations in the demand for gold and to nullify the effect of variations in its supply. Those effects were not completely accomplished, of course, but they were accomplished to a reasonable extent.

The fact that there were financial crises in London during the period from 1846 to 1914 cannot be ignored, but such crises are inevitable to some extent. Such crises as occurred were not prolonged in severity, and they did not run into demoralizing depressions in business. The manner in which the most serious crises, those of 1847, 1857, and 1866, were met is very instructive. When the great demands for money arose at those times, permission from the Government to the Bank of England to expand its Fiduciary Issue allayed the fears. That has been charged against the Bank Charter Act of 1844 as a defect by some, which is intimated by Walter Bagehot's "Lombard Street", but it seems to be more in the nature of proof that the principles upon which the Act was prepared were correct. The fact that a crisis could be met by allowing the Bank to issue more Fiduciary Notes shows that those notes were good sound money. From 1821 to 1914 the pound sterling did not once fail to buy gold at par, a record which has not been equaled by any other major monetary unit of modern times.

CHAPTER V

RETROGRESSION IN THE UNITED STATES

1. ABANDONMENT OF HAMILTON'S SYSTEM

WE have had in the United States four different systems according to which the monetary institutions of the nation have been organized and administered. Since the Hamiltonian System, the first and best one, was abandoned, each succeeding system has been worse than its predecessor. The Jacksonian System, the second best, which was in operation from 1836 to 1861, was as far superior to its successor, which may be called the Chase System, as it was inferior to the organization created by Hamilton. From 1861 until 1913 the Chase System prevailed; and then it was followed by one still worse, the Federal Reserve System — recently revised in a manner which carries the retrogression of a century and a quarter in monetary legislation a step further.

The purpose of this chapter is to review from 1811 to 1914 the course of legislation under which our various kinds of monetary institutions have been created, organized, and administered, inviting attention to the consequences of laws founded upon erroneous principles. In no other nation have monetary laws played such an important part in the lives of the people as in the United States, where those laws have created many unnecessary financial panics, have converted normal recessions in business activity into severe and prolonged depressions, and have caused repeated waves of inflation to be followed by periods of drastic deflation.

One aspect of conditions in the United States, which may no longer exist to such an extent as in the past, must be kept constantly in mind. That is, the great natural resources of the country tended to give rise to many contracts for their development, which in turn gave employment to great numbers of men. At such times the inflationary process, with its course accelerated by the prevailing monetary laws, caused an undue expansion in the making of such contracts; and then everyone was employed, everyone had money, which was considered to be plentiful. A peak in the making of such contracts would always be followed by a period in which fewer new ones would be undertaken and it would become more difficult to perform those for which commitments had been made; and as one project was completed or abandoned its promoters would have no new contracts for the performance of which they would need to employ other men. There would then occur a lack of contracts, a want of jobs, the immediate consequences of which appeared as a scarcity of money. The people would then attempt to reason: "Formerly we had prosperity and a great plentifulness of money together; if Congress would just create some more money, we could be prosperous again." Completely overlooked was the fact that what gave them their money was a contract, and that the very creation of more money was a deterrent to the beginning of new enterprises by one set of men who had to make contracts in order that other men might be employed to perform them. The constantly recurring cry for more money has always been heeded by the politicians, who have not understood the principles applicable.

The beginning of the long backward trend in monetary legislation of the United States was in the refusal of Congress to renew the charter of the Bank of the United States in 1811. That practically destroyed the Hamiltonian System, just as the country was about to enter a war; and that system was pre-eminently qualified for the financing of a war, something it was not called upon to do. The Bank was too efficient as an agent for collection of the notes of state banks, and all who believed in "free banking" joined in persuading Congress not to continue the existence of the Bank. A consequence was that during the War of 1812 the Government sold its bonds for depreciated bank notes, and also was forced to issue Treasury Certificates to circulate as money. These became greatly depreciated, but were not made legal tender. The loss to the Government in selling its bonds for state bank notes is indicated by the facts that with the proceeds of eighty millions in bonds it was able to obtain only thirty-eight millions in coined money, and later had to pay the bonds in good coin. Of course, the prices which the Government had to pay with its notes were higher than in coin. During the war all the banks in the country, except those of New England, were forced to suspend payments in coin. The Bank of the United States, had it been continued, might also have been forced to suspend, but its notes would not have become depreciated to any such extent as that reached by those of the state banks.

After the war was over in 1815, all restraint

upon the formation of state banks was removed. There was one practice of the Government in respect to these banks, begun unfortunately by Hamilton when there were very few banks in the country, which requires attention at this point. That was the receipt of state bank notes in payments due the Government. The fact that taxes and purchases of Government lands could be paid in these bank notes gave them a circulating ability far in excess of what they would have had otherwise, and practically created their inflationary possibilities. These banks were established with little capital except the unpaid subscriptions of their stockholders, for which promissory notes were usually given to the bank. In his "History of American Currency", William Graham Sumner tells of a bank in Rhode Island with such a capital of one million dollars, and when it failed there was in its coffers $86.46 in coin with notes of over half a million outstanding. By 1817, such banks were springing up everywhere — the sparsely settled states of Kentucky, Tennessee, and Ohio having forty-three, ten, and eight respectively. The note issues of all state banks reached the sum of one hundred million dollars. Obviously the acceptance of their notes in payments to the

Government was, under those circumstances, entirely different from what it had been when begun by Hamilton, and the experience of selling bonds at a great loss during the war should have shown the necessity of abandoning the practice at the first opportunity.

That opportunity came with the establishment of the second Bank of the United States by Congress in 1816. The acceptance of state bank notes in payments to the Government was no more than a custom of the Treasury, and could have been stopped by an executive order of either the Secretary of the Treasury or the President. Had the first Bank been continued under the experienced management it had acquired through twenty years of successful operations, it probably would have been able to obtain such an order. But at the beginning of its career the second Bank was placed under political management, and it simply tried to be a rival of the state banks in issuing notes.

The charter of the second Bank was in most respects a copy of the one prepared by Hamilton.[1] Conditions were very different, however, and importantly so in that during the interval of five years

[1] 3 U. S. Statutes at Large 266, April 10, 1816.

between the existence of the two charters the number of state banks had been multiplied many times. The second charter should have contained some provision with respect to bank notes of others than the Bank of the United States, at least forbidding the circulation of those issued by banks which had refused payment in coin. Of course, the correct provision would have been to forbid the issuance of notes by any other bank, but that was impossible under the existing circumstances.

There was in the second charter a departure from Hamilton's principles, in making the note issue of the Bank limited by the amount of its capital, which was thirty-five million dollars. This was a less flexible arrangement than that in the first charter, and was too liberal for the times. Later it might not have been enough, which was a defect not present in the charter of the first Bank, as explained in the third chapter.

One respect in which the charter of the second Bank may have been an improvement upon that of the first was that the Government was permitted to elect a minority of five directors. The percentage of its stockholding in the second Bank was the same as in the first, twenty-five per cent.

With the stage all set for a great inflation, especially after the resumption of payment of bank notes in specie in 1817, the incapable management of the Bank of the United States gave aid to that trend instead of counteracting it. Its excessive note issues contributed to the expansion of the bubble of bank note issues which burst in 1819. After expanding too much at first it later contracted too much, and did very little good of any kind during the first few years of its operation. Its excesses in either expansion or contraction are not to be compared with those of the state banks in both respects.[2] The Panic, or Depression, of 1819 is customarily referred to as a primary post-war one, but in reality it was largely the inevitable collapse of legally created inflation. Escaping from a foolish and disastrous war without having to pay the usual penalties for such incapable statesmanship was enough to start the country upon a wave of prosperity, and indeed did so at first; but the monetary laws of the country helped to convert business opportunities into a wild boom.

When the Bank of the United States was placed under the capable management of Langdon Cheeves,

[2] See Dewey's "Financial History", pp. 144, 149.

who was elected its president in 1819, recovery from the depression began. A conservative policy was adopted and continued, even for some time after Nicholas Biddle succeeded to the presidency of the Bank in 1823. Election of a man the type of Biddle as the chief officer of the Bank was one of this country's greatest misfortunes, as the Bank might have been in existence to-day had that not occurred.[3] Biddle's administration of the affairs of the Bank was reasonably successful until Henry Clay foolishly persuaded him to take the Bank into politics. The record of the two real Central Banks in the United States is best summarized by consideration of the fact that during the forty years of their existence the country was remarkably free from the financial panics which have been so frequent in later years. Of course, the second one has against its record the Depression of 1819 and the financial disturbances attendant upon its death struggle with President Jackson. The events of neither period, however, are to be regarded as normal for institutions of the kind; those of 1819 having occurred before the

---

[3] Biddle's career after the Bank's charter expired in 1836 seems to justify this statement. See William Graham Sumner's Essay on "The Commercial Crisis of 1837."

Bank's management acquired experience and while
it was in the hands of political appointees, and those
in the closing years of its career under circumstances
which capable statesmen never would have permitted
to arise. De Tocqueville commented favorably upon
the fact that he found the notes of the second Bank
circulating at par in all sections of the country.[4]
How many times since then has any well-informed
and observant foreigner commented upon the excellence of the organization of monetary institutions
in the United States?

About the time of the beginning of the attack of
President Jackson upon the Bank, Congress made
another marked departure from the Hamiltonian
System. From 1792 until 1834 the Mint Act had
remained in effect without alteration, and the country
had had its trade facilitated by the circulation of
subsidiary coins, except to some extent during the
days of bank suspensions. Those coins had been of
silver all along, as explained in the third chapter,
and there was no gold in circulation. Probably some
of the members of Congress decided "to do something for gold", as they raised its price from 24.75
grains pure per dollar to 23.22 grains per dollar.

[4] "Democracy in America", Vol. 1, p. 526.

No one at the time would give 371.25 pure grains of silver for 23.22 grains of gold, and as those quantities of each metal respectively would bring only one dollar at the Mint, silver was withdrawn from circulation to melt and sell as bullion. The country then automatically shifted from a silver to a gold standard, and the result was that all the small coins disappeared from circulation. No provision had been made in the original Mint Act for coining any gold piece of less value than two dollars and one half, and that Act prescribed that dimes, quarters, and half-dollars should be made of silver in quantities of proper proportions to that in dollars. Congress failed to amend the law in this respect, overlooking the fact that the new price for gold overvalued that metal, and that in order to retain small change it would be necessary to have a system of token coins.

The retail trade of the country was then seriously inconvenienced, as there was a gap in small change from the nickel to the two-dollar-and-a-half gold piece. There was, in the charter of the Bank of the United States, a prohibition against its issuing any note for less than five dollars; and some of the states had laws to the same effect applying to their banks. The great want of small change offered an excuse for the issuance of bank notes of lesser denominations, and most of the states which had laws forbidding that repealed them. Thus the way was opened for a grand inflation, with state bank notes, just before another check upon the abuse of that privilege was about to be removed by refusing to continue the existence of the Bank of the United States. A state bank was comparatively safe in issuing excessive amounts of notes for two dollars and less.

In view of the long-prevailing difficulties in England with subsidiary coins, under similar circumstances, with gold being overvalued by law, and the Act of Parliament in 1816 which made those coins tokens, it is hard to understand why such men as Webster, Calhoun, and Clay failed to point out the consequences of this Act of Congress in 1834. Had it been pointed out, both President Jackson and Senator Thomas H. Benton — who detested paper money so thoroughly that he came to be called "old Bullion" — would have been delighted to amend the law by decreasing the silver content of subsidiary coins so that they would have remained in circulation to compete with state bank notes. This all shows that the excellence of Hamilton's System was not then either understood or properly appreciated, as indeed it has not been to this day. After other nations learned to do what Hamilton first did for this country, we ignorantly abandoned the benefits of the great organization of monetary institutions with which he started the nation on the road to prosperity.

2. THE JACKSONIAN SYSTEM

The subject here is not so much how President Jackson came to establish his system as it is the principles upon which he proceeded. There are, however, certain aspects of the situation at the time President Jackson was inaugurated to which attention should be invited.

Sumner says that Jackson "had imbibed from what he had seen of paper money in Tennessee and Kentucky, a fierce but not too intelligent detestation of it." [5] All, or at least by far the greater part, of that unsatisfactory experience had been with state bank notes, and not with notes of either Bank of the United States. It seems almost certain that Jackson did not go into office in 1828 with the determination not to permit renewal of the Bank's charter in

[5] "History of American Currency", p. 92.

1836. His hostility against paper money might easily have been directed to state bank notes had a man of a type different from Biddle been at the head of the Bank, and if the friends of the Bank had had intelligence enough not to make a political issue of the renewal of its charter. When Henry Clay was foolish enough to run for President against Jackson in 1832 and make renewal of the Bank's charter his proposal, he not only put Jackson on the opposite side, but almost forced him to take the position that his re-election was a mandate from the people not to permit the Bank's charter to be continued. Furthermore, the Bank was very unwise with respect to some of its relations with public officers.[6] It must not be forgotten that Congress once passed a bill renewing the charter of the Bank, and Jackson vetoed it.

Biddle — whether intentionally or not, certainly very unwisely — permitted an expansion of the Bank's note issues; and then began a program of drastic contraction, which caused many financial hardships. That gave Jackson an opportunity to represent the Bank as a "Monster" making and destroying paper money to serve its own ends to the dis-

[6] Fuess, "Daniel Webster", Vol. II, pp. 7, 13.

advantage of the people. Jackson's sincerity cannot be questioned, and he is regarded by many as a reformer of the currency, with a desire to substitute a sound one for questionable paper.[7]

Although some efforts had been made to prevent the undue acceptance of state bank notes in payments to the Government, Jackson's beginning to make Treasury deposits of money in state banks instead of continuing the Treasury deposits with the Bank of the United States gave great encouragement to the expansion of state bank notes. The so-called "Pet Banks", through the Government's deposits, were given additional resources with which to create inflation. Thus as the existence of the Bank of the United States was about to terminate, both that Bank and those of the states were actively inflating — the former expecting, if its charter was not renewed, to become a state bank, when it also would no longer be restrained from issuing notes for less than five dollars. Sales of Government lands in the West were at the rate of approximately twenty-five millions a year, and this gave great inflationary force to the Eastern banks, which could issue notes

[7] He is so mentioned in "History of the Bank of England", Andréadès, pp. 265, 267.

for that purpose with the certainty that they could not be presented for payment before several months had elapsed.

The most obvious first step in the beginning of Jackson's efforts to create a new system of monetary institutions was to issue orders against any further Treasury acceptance of state bank notes. That should have been done before the absurd mistake of amending the Mint Act was made, and also before the Treasury began to deposit its money in those banks. The failure to issue such an order at least as soon as immediately after the election in 1832, when it became apparent that the charter of the Bank of the United States would not be renewed, gave the inflation four years in which to reach a peak far too high. A brief summary of the inflationary aspects of the situation is as follows: the Government was encouraging the expansion of bank notes by accepting them in payments due to it; then the subsidiary coins of the country were destroyed, leaving a gap between five cents and two dollars and a half, to be filled with state bank notes; the Government began to deposit its money in selected state banks, which added to their inflationary capacity; and finally the great agency for the collection of state bank notes, the Bank of the United States, was about to be removed from the field.

The Panic of 1837 cannot be charged against the Jacksonian System, as it was not completely developed at the time, and certainly not against that of Hamilton, as it had been completely abandoned before the Panic came. When the inflation was at its greatest height, the most sound part of the paper currency, the notes of the Bank of the United States, were destroyed by refusing to renew the Bank's charter. This action was followed by another foolish one of Congress — that of distributing to the States a surplus which had accumulated in the National Treasury. Further inflationary capacities were given to state banks by this action. The states themselves began to establish banks which were mere agencies for the emission of notes. This was in clear violation of the Constitution, which says "No State shall . . . emit Bills of credit", and had been so declared, at least inferentially, by Chief Justice Marshall.[8] The only logical meaning of this provision in the Constitution is that a state may not incorporate a bank and authorize it to issue bank notes, as a state cannot do indirectly what the Constitution forbids it

[8] Craig *v*. Missouri, 4 Peters 410.

to do directly. When a case involving the notes of a state-chartered and state-owned bank reached the Supreme Court, the great Chief Justice was gone, and the Court proceeded to overrule him.[9]

All these actions and omissions of the Govern-

[9] Briscoe v. Bank of Kentucky, 11 Peters 257. That Chief Justice Marshall, in writing the opinion in Craig v. Missouri (Craig v. Missouri, 4 Peters 410, pp. 432, 433) understood the question involved is shown by the following extracts from his opinion: —

What is the character of the certificates issued by authority of the act under consideration? What office are they to perform? Certificates signed by the auditor and treasurer of the State, are to be issued by those officers to the amount of two hundred thousand dollars, of denominations not exceeding ten dollars, nor less than fifty cents. The paper purports on its face to be receivable at the treasury, or at any loan-office of the State of Missouri, in discharge of taxes or debts due to the State.

The law makes them receivable in discharge of all taxes or debts due to the State, or any county or town therein; and of all salaries and fees of office, to all officers civil and military within the State; and for salt sold by the lessees of the public salt-works. It also pledges the faith and funds of the State for their redemption.

It seems impossible to doubt the intention of the legislature in passing this act, or to mistake the character of these certificates, or the office they were to perform. The denominations of the bills, from ten dollars to fifty cents, fitted them for the purpose of ordinary circulation; and their reception in payment of taxes, and debts to the government and to corporations, and of salaries and fees, would give them currency. They were to be put into circulation; that is, emitted, by the government. In addition to all these evidences of an intention to make these certificates the ordinary circulating medium of the country, the law speaks of them in this character, and directs the auditor and treasurer to withdraw annually one tenth of them from circulation.

In the opinion in Briscoe v. Bank (*Supra,* pp. 317, 318) there is the following passage: —

ment brought the inflation to a great peak, and the Government itself demolished the superstructure which its laws had caused. President Jackson caused to be issued, in July 1836, the famous Specie Circular, forbidding any further acceptance of bank notes in payments to the Government. The order should have been given twenty years sooner, and had it been issued at the beginning of Jackson's first Administration, or even of the second one, it would have gone far toward preventing the Panic of 1837. As conditions were, however, the Specie Circular caused the collapse of the state banks.

That by the constitution, the currency, so far as it is composed of gold and silver, is placed under the exclusive control of congress, is clear; and it is contended, from the inhibition on the States to emit bills of credit, that the paper medium was intended to be made subject to the same power.

If this argument be correct, and the position that a State cannot do indirectly what it is prohibited from doing directly, be a sound one, then it must follow, as a necessary consequence, that all banks incorporated by a State are unconstitutional. And this, in the printed argument, is earnestly maintained, though it is admitted not to be necessary to sustain the ground assumed for the plaintiffs. The counsel of the plaintiffs, who have argued the case at the bar, do not carry the argument to this extent.

This doctrine is startling, as it strikes a fatal blow against the state banks, which have a capital of near $400,000,000, and which supply almost the entire circulating medium of the country.

The opinion in the latter case attempted to distinguish a note issued by a bank wholly owned by the State of Kentucky from a bill of credit.

A wave of bank failures occurred, and those which did not close suspended payment of their notes. The misery of the people in being subjected to widespread unemployment and bankruptcies during the Depression of 1837 forms no part of the present subject, as the purpose here is to invite attention to the course of Government in establishing a new system of monetary institutions. Those actions were incidentally, but necessarily, the cause of the Panic, and to describe that as either a secondary post-war depression or as due to overexpansion in industry and speculation in canals, internal improvements, and lands, is to ignore the real cause. The speculation, like the overexpansion, was the result of inflation created by law, and the deflation which followed was just as certainly caused by legal means.

No better proof of the contention that the power to create money is a part of the power to collect taxes is needed than the events which led up to the Panic of 1837. They may be summarized in chronological order as follows: —

1. Permitting state banks to issue notes.
2. Accepting such notes in payments to the Government.

3. Destruction of the subsidiary coinage by the amendment to the Mint Act in 1834.
4. Depositing Government money in state banks.
5. Distribution of the Treasury surplus to the states, following the Act of June, 1836.
6. The Specie Circular, July 1836.

To the above list might be added the refusal to renew the charter of the Bank of the United States, which was allowed to expire in the first part of 1836. The relations between the state bank notes and the Specie Circular are especially important in considering the nature of money. The banks had little of either gold or silver, and were almost entirely dependent upon Government support for the expansion of their note issues. The severe contraction in their note issues was not caused by loss of gold, but by the withdrawal of Government support. By the adoption of an erroneous principle the Government, almost unconsciously, by accepting state bank notes had created what was in effect a large amount of money. Then, again without comprehending fully the nature of its act, it practically destroyed that money by refusing to accept it any longer. The money was created by saying that it could be used

165

to pay taxes, and destroyed by the withdrawal of that privilege.

The actions commented upon above were all that were ever taken by President Jackson toward completion of his system. That was simple, and may be briefly described. The only money, ordinarily in circulation, was coined gold, pieces of five cents in nickel, and copper pennies. Bank notes were mere private promises to pay money, without regulation or support of the National Government, except so far as it deposited money in certain banks. The credit of the Government was used in no way in the creation of money. There was no Central Bank to buy and sell the precious metals for the purposes of commerce with other nations, which was a serious deficiency. The only activities of the National Government in the creation of money were in coining such gold as was brought to the Mint, and nickels and pennies.

Steps which were ultimately taken to complete the Jacksonian System were the establishment of a Subtreasury method of handling the Government's money, and the adoption of a token coinage for dimes, quarters, and half-dollars. The former, begun in Van Buren's Administration, then temporarily abandoned but re-established in 1846, removed the last of governmental aids to inflation with bank notes. In beginning a system of token coinage of silver, — which was not done until 1853, however, — the great mistake of the Amendment to the Mint Act in 1834 was repaired. After these two changes were made the Jacksonian System was on a firm foundation, but had three great defects. Those were: it lacked the necessary arrangements for facilitating exchanges with foreign nations; there was no provision whatsoever for any aid to Government financing in an emergency; state bank notes were left entirely free from adequate regulation, and the states were allowed to give them one aid to inflationary possibilities. The last requires some explanation.

Any ordinary business institution which made a contract to pay money, and, on proper demand, failed to perform it, was subject to execution of a judgment rendered against it by a court, in which event the sheriff would take possession and sell its assets unless payment was forthcoming. Banks, however, were frequently regarded as being immune from such process of the law, and so general was their exemption that they might confidently assume that a suspension of the payment of bank notes in specie would not mean a suspension of business. To close a bank because it refused to pay its notes seems to have been comparatively rare.[10] This fault was largely attributable to the carelessness and neglect of the states, but it was a part of the system which should have received the attention of the National Government. The banks would not have been nearly so free in issuing notes had this defect not existed.

In one respect Jackson's System of hard money only was well adapted to the conditions of the country. At the time, agriculture was the predominant industry, and one of its greatest enemies is inflation. Even a moderate use of Government credit in the creation of money causes some inflation, from which the farmers in a country that exports a large surplus of agricultural products cannot benefit. The price of that surplus, as well as to some extent that of the part of agricultural production which is consumed internally, is determined by its exchange abroad for gold. So long as the inflation does not go far enough to raise the price of gold, the farmer sees it carry upward the prices of all things which

[10] Sumner, in his "History of American Currency", comments on this extensively.

he buys, without so moving the prices of what he sells. This is especially true when there is a protective tariff to prevent the farmer from buying goods abroad with the gold which he receives for his exports. If he can bring the goods in, the fact that their price has risen internally does not hurt him, but when he is forced to bring in gold only, and sell that at a price which remains fixed, a loss falls upon him in buying the other goods he needs. Without doubt the Jacksonian System, by preventing any great amount of inflation from 1837 to 1861, — during the period of its entire life in fact, — conferred great benefits upon the farmers of the United States.

There is an important contrast between the Systems of Hamilton and Jackson. The former used Government credit in the creation of money on principles which were as near to being completely correct as could have been expected at the time; while the latter used Government credit in no way. The choice must be one of the two extremes. There should be no use of Government credit in the creation of money if the correct principle is not followed, and it never has been in the United States since the time Hamilton's System was abandoned. That is the reason the System established by Jackson was so far superior to any of its successors.

The Panic of 1857 gave the Jacksonian System a thorough test, and it met the test better than would have been done by any system we have had since that time. State banks had succeeded by 1857 in causing some inflation, although it did not begin to compare in extent with that of either 1836 or 1929. The country recovered from that depression with remarkable speed, which was due largely to the facts that there had been almost no legal aids to inflation preceding the Panic, which was less severe on that account, and that there was no resort to such expedients to try to get out of the ensuing depression.

One of the System's great defects was the direct cause of abandoning the Jacksonian System almost at the outbreak of the Civil War. It was utterly incapable of standing the strain of financing a war of any magnitude, although it had served very well for the small Mexican affair. That the Jacksonian System was a retrogression from that of Hamilton may hardly be denied, but fair treatment demands that it be said that the degree by which it excelled any System we have since had far exceeds that by which it fell below its predecessor.

3. THE CHASE SYSTEM

There was available, at the time the National Government was confronted with the burden of financing a great war, one plain and adequate remedy for the existing deficiencies in the monetary institutions of the country. That was the re-enactment of the original charter of the Bank of the United States, with possibly some expansion of the limitation upon the amount of its Fiduciary Issue of notes. As most of the banks had suspended payment of their notes within a short time after commencement of the war, and the Government could hardly hope to use the state banks as satisfactory fiscal agents, it was obvious to the new Secretary of the Treasury, Salmon P. Chase, that some changes in the prevailing monetary system had to be made. He was unequal to the task, however, and while he neglected an opportunity, which was nearly as great as the one seized by Hamilton, Congress proceeded to create the notorious "greenbacks." Those were Government notes promising to pay coined dollars, with no prospect of the promise being good until the emergency was over. The practice of issuing Treasury certificates, both interest-bear-

171

ing and without interest, had been followed previously by the National Government, but such paper had not been declared to be legal tender in private payments, as were the greenbacks. One grossly unfair feature of this legislation was that the Government proposed to pay its soldiers in this kind of paper money, but the Government itself refused to accept it in the payment of all taxes. Naturally the notes quickly became depreciated, and added greatly to the cost of the war. Had greenbacks been made receivable in all payments to the Government, and a vigorous attempt made to collect adequate taxes, greenbacks would not have depreciated to the extent reached, which was the requirement of two-and-one-half dollars of that kind for one gold dollar.

This greenback law was the first step in adding to the currency system of the country various confusing kinds of money, one created on one theory and the next on another theory, with no controlling principle in the minds of any of the legislators. It was the second mistake of important historical consequences in the monetary legislation of the United States, the first having occurred when Congress refused to renew the charter of the first Bank of the United States in 1811. Had that Bank been continued in existence through the War of 1812, the fiscal operations of the Government would have been conducted on a basis so much sounder than the usual one of nations at war that the institution would have acquired a prestige sufficient to carry it through the years with a management constantly growing wiser from experience. Biddle never would have become the President of such an institution, no war between it and the Government could have occurred, greenbacks would never have been heard of, and all the idiotic experiments with money since undertaken in this country would not have disgraced its history.

Also, the greenback legislation represented the first definite departure from the provisions of the Constitution on the subject of money. That was in the part of the Act which made them legal tender in private payments. This presents a subject worthy of some consideration, especially in view of recent legislation, such as the Gold Clause Resolution of Congress in 1933. The consequences of the neglect of principles written into the Constitution first appear, from a practical view, with the legal-tender provisions used with reference to the greenbacks. Up to this point, in considering the application of the Constitution to laws relating to money and banking, it has been sufficient to regard the taxing clause as giving to Congress all necessary powers over both kinds of laws. The power to declare legal tender is not one of necessity, however, and proper consideration of that subject requires that reference be made to other clauses of the Constitution.

Those clauses are: —

The Congress shall have Power:

To borrow Money on the credit of the United States;

To coin Money, regulate the Value thereof, and of foreign Coin;

To make all Laws which shall be necessary and proper for carrying into Execution the foregoing Powers. (Article I, Section 8.)

No State shall . . . coin Money; emit Bills of Credit; make any Thing but gold and silver Coin a Tender in Payment of Debts; pass any . . . Law impairing the Obligation of Contracts. (Article I, Section 10.)

The powers not delegated to the United States by the Constitution, nor prohibited by it to the States, are reserved to the States respectively, or to the people. (Tenth Amendment.)

So far as the law of legal tender is concerned, the plain and logical meaning of the provisions quoted above is simply this: Congress has no power to declare any kind of money, whether it be gold, silver, or paper, to be legal tender in private payments; but any kind of gold or silver coin issued by authority of Congress is legal tender. The practical effect is that the law of legal tender is written into the Constitution, and may not be altered by legislation, either of Congress or of the States. These propositions would require no argument if the Supreme Court had not held to the contrary, but all the opinions on this subject of legal tender have proceeded upon the assumption that Congress has power by legislation to make gold and silver coin legal tenders in private payments, which is begging the question. Certainly Congress has the power to declare what is legal tender in all payments either to or by the National Government, and that is sufficient.

It is significant that, when the clause relating to borrowing money came before the Convention in the form "to borrow Money and emit Bills on the Credit of the United States", the three words "and emit Bills" were stricken out. Madison's explanation was that "striking out the words would not disable the Government from the use of public notes, so far as they could be safe and proper, and would only cut off the pretext for a paper currency, and particularly for making the bills a tender, either for public or private debts." [11] In other words, the authority to issue bills was in the Constitution by virtue of the tax clause. Evidently both Madison and Hamilton understood that the precious metals, even when in form bearing the Mint's certificate of weight and fineness, were things which would command a price in "Bills of Credit." It is to be noticed also that the clause, "to coin money, regulate the value thereof", makes no mention either of any kind of metal out of which the coins should be made, or of any kind of tender. The joining of the metals and tender with contracts in Article One, Section Ten, is significant. John Marshall said that the power to declare legal tender "resided in the States" at the time the Constitution was adopted.[12] There is no provision in the Constitution which takes that power from the states, and confers it upon Congress. The clause "No State shall make any Thing but gold and silver Coin a Tender in Payment of Debts" must be given some meaning. If Congress has power to make "any Thing" a tender in payment of *private* debts, the clause can have almost no meaning, and

[11] See Dewey's "Financial History", p. 67.
[12] Craig *v.* Missouri, 4 Peters 410, at 435.

is wasteful language. Here was an important power which "resided in the States", and they were limited in its exercise, but no part of the power was directly given to Congress. The question is neither what was the intended meaning nor what meaning has been ascribed by judicial construction. The Constitution must be construed according to the actual meaning of the language used. In the case of a statute, the fact that the legislature allows it to remain in effect as interpreted by the courts is sufficient to make the judicial construction effective as if it were a part of the statute, but that is not true of a constitution. Therefore, it is reasonable to question the accuracy of the Legal Tender decisions about the greenbacks, since the Court gave no attention to the provision of the Constitution quoted above.

When all the provisions of the Constitution which relate to contracts, money, and banking are considered together, it seems to appear clearly that the Convention regarded the law of legal tender as a part of the law of contracts, which view was correct. It becomes important, therefore, to determine the manner in which the Constitution deals with the law of contracts. The members of the Convention had a thorough comprehension of the functions which contracts perform, and their work indicates that they properly considered contracts to be of more importance than money. A complete and accurate survey of the field of the law of contracts was made, and the lines dividing it between the National Government and the states were precisely drawn.

The Convention found the states in possession of all power over the law of contracts, and proceeded to deal with that power on the same general principle used for all others. That principle was to grant powers to the National Government, either directly or by implication, and to treat the remainder of sovereign powers as reserved to the states. One important specific grant concerning the law of contracts was made to Congress, which was the authority to enact uniform bankruptcy laws. A bankruptcy law, in giving the bankrupt a discharge from debts, permits the obligation of contracts to be impaired. This was the only specific grant to Congress of power over the law of contracts, and the fact that a specific grant was considered necessary shows that, in general, Congress was not to be permitted to legislate concerning that law. Also, in the same connection, it is significant that the Convention rejected a proposal to forbid Congress to pass any law impairing the obligation of contracts, of which the generally accepted explanation is that such a limitation was considered unnecessary, as Congress could not legislate concerning private contracts.

The two great limitations imposed upon the states, so far as their power over the law of contracts was concerned, were in the provisions about legal tender and impairing the obligation of contracts. A difference in the language used in the two clauses is important. The first forbids a state "to *make*" any "Thing" except gold and silver coin a tender; while the second forbids a state "to *pass*" any law impairing the obligation of contracts. Judicial as well as legislative action is covered by the first, but the second obviously applies to legislative action only. In other words, no State Court may render a decision saying that anything other than gold and silver coin is a tender in payment of debts — which puts it beyond the power of Congress to enact a law requiring a State Court to hold that any kind of paper money is legal tender. When a case arising out of a contract is tried in a court of the United States, the first task of that court is to determine what states' law applies to the contract, and then give the contract effect according to that law. Obviously when the Constitution says no State Court shall render a decision making paper money legal tender, the Supreme Court may not reverse on appeal and direct that such a judgment shall be given. Since the states determine the law of contracts, the practical effect of the Constitution is that no kind of money except gold and silver coin shall be a tender in payment of private debts.

The effect of the clause goes beyond that, however, as it practically states the law of legal tender in private payments. It forbids the states as well as Congress to legislate on the subject. All power over money is taken from the states. Consequently, they may not deny the attribute of being legal tender to any gold or silver coin issued by authority of Congress. In regulating the value of coined money Congress may debase it, but that will not prevent it from being legal tender.

Unfortunately, a trend away from the Constitution was begun almost with the first monetary legislation. The Mint Act of 1792 provided that the coins authorized should be legal tender in all payments "whatsoever." That was entirely unnecessary, as both gold and silver were then precious metals, and were what everyone was striving to obtain. Was that provision an unconscious usurpation of power by Hamilton, or was it intended to include only those payments over which Congress had jurisdiction? The origin of the assumption that Congress has power to declare coined money to be legal tender is perhaps attributable to that section of the statute.

With respect to banking also there had long been a trend away from the Constitution. As has been previously observed, the states had no power whatsoever to incorporate banks and authorize them to issue bank notes, which was to "emit Bills of Credit", something the states themselves were forbidden to do. The course of development, if according to the Constitution, would have been for the Bank of the United States to become the head of a system of national banks, gradually driving out the state banks. Through an erroneous construction of the Constitution, the state banks were permitted to force the discontinuance of a national bank. The departure from the principles of constitutional law promulgated by Hamilton and Marshall had many serious consequences, one of which was that in a financial crisis induced by war there were no banks which could serve the fiscal purposes of the Government.

It was unfortunate that the primary purpose of the establishment of a system of national banks should have been that of aiding in the sale of Government bonds, although that was a proper incidental purpose. Secretary of the Treasury Chase, who was largely responsible for the establishment during the war of a system of independent national banks, seems to have thought that he was going back to the principles of Hamilton — which was far from the case, however. It is interesting to observe that, on the first partial departure from Hamilton's System, it required only five years to see the wisdom of returning to it; while on the second, which was complete, it required twenty-four years to produce an attempt to supply the deficiencies created. The new plan was to provide for the incorporation of small and independent national banks, and to authorize them to issue bank notes on the security of Government bonds. These notes were made acceptable in payments to the Government generally, but there were some important exceptions, as in the case of greenbacks. In amount they were limited at first to one hundred and fifty million dollars, but later that sum was increased.

Thus there was added another confusing feature to the monetary system of the country. National bank notes were payable in what was called "lawful money" of the United States, — as if there could be any other kind, — which meant that they were payable in greenbacks. More and more the country was denying to itself any satisfactory arrangements for commerce with other nations. Under the Jacksonian System, all banks were supposed to pay their notes in coined gold, according to the law, and then the gold coins might be shipped abroad for sale as bullion. But now an obstruction and cause of uncertainty in foreign exchanges was introduced, as a call upon a bank for gold might be met by a tender of greenbacks, which had been issued as a promise to deliver gold by a National Treasury which had none. This was of no significance so long as the depreciation of the currency continued during the financial crisis of the war, but the defect remained long after the emergency had passed. Introduction of the greenbacks and national bank notes caused the Government of the United States to become a dealer in gold, which was a calamity that has brought untold misery to its people. Here was a defect in the Chase System which had not been present in the system of either Hamilton or Jackson. Making the Government a dealer in gold has played a great part in causing the adoption by Congress of every one of the fallacious theories about money which have been enacted into law since 1865.

The whole idea of issuing bank notes on the security of Government bonds was fallacious. It had been borrowed from the state of New York, which required state banks issuing notes to maintain on deposit with one of its officials a sufficient amount of the state's bonds to secure payment of the notes, and that was clearly in violation of the Constitution. The great defect in the national use of such a system was that when the Government was heavily in debt and had large amounts of bonds outstanding national bank notes might be made comparatively plentiful: but should the Government pay off its debt, then there would have to be a contraction of the currency whether it was advisable or not. Later this very situation arose to the great disadvantage of the country.

Another great mistake made with the Chase System was the establishment of a new kind of bank to compete with a kind already in existence. This was another defect which had not been present in either of the two preceding systems. At first the national banks were not by any means as successful in their competition with state banks as had been expected. The war had caused a revival in the belief that the power of the National Government should be nearer that contemplated by Hamilton and Marshall than to the theories of Jefferson and Jackson. There was a great opportunity to prevent competition between two systems of banks, one under national control and the other under that of the states. That opportunity was lost through ignorance of the legal nature of the banking business. There can be no doubt that the Act of 1866 was intended to pass a sentence of death upon state banks. Instead of forbidding any bank other than a national bank to make a contract to pay money on demand, which was the purpose to be accomplished, the Act imposed a tax of ten per cent. upon any bank which paid out a bank note issued by a state bank or any one other than a national bank.

A bank note is only one kind of physical evidence of the existence of a contract to pay money on demand, being the banker's statement that the contract has been made and will be performed upon proper demand, which is the presentation of the note. That is a very convenient form of the evidence for circulating purposes, but there is another form of evidence of the contract's existence, which is almost equally convenient for circulation. The latter is the statement of the one with whom the banker made the contract, and may be to the same purport as that expressed in the bank note, only in the second instance the statement is legally implied from the drawing of an order on the bank to perform the contract, or a part of it. This shift from the use of bank notes to that of checks had occurred in England as the result of legislation there in 1833 and 1844, and the lesson should have been learned from that instead of having to be learned from actual experience. The state banks simply ceased to issue notes, and, by resorting to the use of checks, continued to make and perform contracts to pay on demand, the business of commercial banking from which the intention was to exclude them. If Congress had the power to prevent the circulation of one kind of evidence of the existence of such a contract, as it was held to have by the Supreme Court,[18] then the circu-

[18] Veazie Bank *v*. Fenno, 8 Wallace 533.

lation of any other kind of physical evidence of the same fact could have been prevented just as easily. The intention of Congress was to remove this weakness in the system, but failure to comprehend the legal nature of the problem left the country suffering from competition between two kinds of banks, each subject to a different regulatory power. State banks acquired a new lease on life; the opportunity to correct the defect slipped away, and did not return until 1933, when it was again neglected.

After the war expenditures ceased, it was inevitable that all the inflation created by the emergency financing and the new monetary laws should collapse. There was much confusion as to the legal tender qualities of the greenbacks in peace time, especially as to whether they were a good tender for debts incurred before they were issued. At first the Supreme Court held that they were not,[14] and later that they were.[15] Also Congress decided soon after the war to restrict the issue of greenbacks and to try to bring them to par, but the cry for more money was too powerful a political factor for that to be

[14] Hepburn v. Griswold, 8 Wallace 603.
[15] Knox v. Lee, 12 Wallace 457.

accomplished. So more greenbacks were issued. The currency was depreciated and fluctuating for some time while the country grew up to the amount of money that had been created.

Before greenbacks became able to buy gold at par, another important law was enacted with the usual unhappy results. It is to be remembered that the original Mint Act had been amended only in 1834, and that either silver or gold could be coined into money at the Mint, the former at the rate of 371.25 grains per dollar and the latter at 23.22. As the open-market price of 371.25 grains of silver had ever since 1834 remained higher than that of 23.22 grains of gold, no silver had been coined during all that time. For some reason Congress decided to revise the Mint Act, and in doing so omitted the provision for the free coinage of silver. At the time neither greenbacks nor national bank notes would buy either 23.22 grains of gold per dollar or 371.25 grains of silver. But the Act of 1873 was passed just before some of the nations of Europe began to try to copy the British gold standard, and as that occurred, perhaps along with other reasons, the price of silver began to fall. When it fell below 371.25 grains per dollar, which happened about

1876, the Act of 1873, having attracted little attention at the time of its passage, began to be denounced as a surreptitious "demonetization" of silver, and as the "Crime of 1873."

As greenbacks were gradually approaching par with gold in 1876, and the fall in the price of silver would soon have shifted the country back to a silver standard, it would have been far better to have permitted that to occur, by silver going to the Mint for coinage because it was worth in the open market less than 371.25 grains per dollar of greenbacks, than to inject the silver question as a perpetual source of annoyance in the monetary problems of the United States. The controversy about the free coinage of silver has disturbed this country from 1876 until 1896, and from 1930 until the present. Probably that has done far greater harm than would have come from shifting to a silver standard in 1876 and remaining on it until this day. The latter would not have occurred, however, as there undoubtedly would have been, other circumstances remaining the same, several shifts back and forth from one metal to the other. Possibly the public would have become tired of the fluctuation, and forced the adoption of a workable gold standard, which was not created by either the Act of 1873 or any subsequent legislation.

It is of importance to understand the causes for the repeated disturbances in the United States due to the controversy over the silver question. The substantial results of legislation "to do something for silver" are simply a subsidy to silver miners and a loss to all other citizens. It seems that there never has been sufficient political strength in the demands for the subsidy to enable that alone to accomplish the purpose, but such forces must always receive aid from other motives. The great source of the ability of advocates of "doing something for silver" to incorporate their desires in the monetary laws of the country is always to be found in the defects in those laws existing at the time the cry for the "remonetization of silver" arises. This may be easily demonstrated.

The Government buys gold. Why should it not also buy silver? If the Government had never commenced dealing in gold, there would have been little force behind the demand that it deal in silver. Here emphasis must be given the statement previously made, that the Government was not a dealer in either, under the systems of Hamilton and Jackson, as it made no promises to deliver, or sell, them, but merely offered free coinage at a specified rate to anyone who brought either metal to the Mint. To repeat again, the great defect of the Chase System lay in the fact that when the Government began to issue, in the form of greenbacks, promises to deliver gold, when it had none, and if it ever redeemed those promises it would be forced to become a dealer in gold, unless it accumulated the total amount involved and paid off all greenbacks at once. As the demand for greenbacks as a means of paying taxes and other debts increased, the Government, by acquiring some gold and selling it for greenbacks, — the most natural way of dealing with the immediate problem of "resumption of specie payments", as it was somewhat erroneously called, — inevitably became a dealer in gold. It was, after January 1, 1879, a dealer in gold alone, and not silver, by virtue of the Act of 1873. If there had been in existence at the commencement of the Civil War the Bank of the United States, its note issue would undoubtedly have been expanded, and there would have been some depreciation of its notes: but the Government would not have become a dealer in gold. The Bank probably would have been relieved of its obligation to sell gold at a fixed price, but would have dealt in it at fluctuating prices, and undoubtedly would have restored its notes to par long before 1879. Now the silver miners could not have demanded a subsidy from a Bank of the United States, a private institution. Furthermore, such a Bank would have had the option of delivering either coined gold or silver in redemption of its notes, and would have objected strenuously to being deprived of the benefit of that advantage in times so precarious financially as 1873, which probably would have been sufficient to prevent the Act of 1873. Being on a gold instead of a silver standard from 1879 until 1933 certainly did not confer enough benefits on the country to offset the damage done by the silver controversy.

There was another defect in the Chase System which gave to the silver advocates a great part of their strength by enabling them to obtain allies to an extent otherwise impossible. By 1879 greenbacks had become definitely limited in amount, unless expanded by Act of Congress, and National Bank Notes could not be expanded without Government bonds to serve as security for their issuance. As the Government paid off its war debt those bonds became scarce, and the consequence was national bank notes were decreased in amount. The country had grown up to the currency inflation of war times, and there should have been arrangements by which there could be some expansion of the currency on demand, as there were no banking reserve arrangements whatever; but instead there was contraction when production and national wealth were growing. Since greenbacks could not be expanded, and national bank notes were decreasing, the only possible way to extend the currency was through the coinage of gold. The defects in the monetary system made the United States an unsafe place for the deposit of gold, as there was the probability that both greenbacks and national bank notes might become depreciated again at almost any time, and this was especially true in view of the agitations for both the issuance of more greenbacks and the free coinage of silver. Should Congress resort to either remedy, and it was constantly on the verge of doing either or both, it would be impossible to buy gold with either kind of paper currency at par. Therefore, gold would not come in sufficiently to meet the demands for more money, which for once had some reason behind them. The elements of reason in those demands made many allies for the advocates of silver legislation, and were to a great extent responsible for giving the latter strength enough to insist that their remedy was the only one.

Thus the very existence of two serious defects in the monetary system of the country served to bring in a third one, and add confusion to complication. The first Act for the coinage of silver, at the expense of the people and for the benefit of silver miners, was passed in 1876. It required the Treasury to buy not less than two and not more than four million dollars worth of silver per month, and to coin it into legal tender dollars. When the Government became able to meet its promises to sell gold at 23.22 grains of gold per dollar of greenbacks, this silver law put it at great disadvantage. In trying to stay on an awkward and poorly designed gold standard, the Government was forced to sell gold for these silver dollars. Since the latter were too cumbersome for ordinary circulation the use of silver certificates was adopted. This was another complication added to an already confused system.

A different silver purchase Act was passed in 1890 to require that the Treasury buy, with legal-tender notes issued for the purpose, four-and-one-half million ounces of silver each month. This Act also expressed the policy of the United States as being to maintain the two metals at parity with each other, the idea of parity being that the Treasury should sell 23.22 grains of gold for a dollar and buy 371.25 grains of silver at the same price. There was an utter failure to understand that the Standard of International Trade was set by Great Britain, and that the United States was then without power to affect that standard. The only choice was that the foreign commerce of the United States might be conveniently conducted on a gold standard, or inconveniently, and more expensively, conducted on a silver standard. At that time it was absurd to suppose that the Government could continue to sell gold at the price established in 1834, and at the same time buy silver at a price ranging from twenty-five to one hundred per cent. above that of the open market. Either the selling of gold or the buying of silver had to be abandoned, and the fear that it would be the former played a great part in bringing on the Panic and depression of 1893. Finally, in October of that year, President Cleveland induced Congress to repeal the silver purchase Act. The demands for the free coinage of silver at the ratio of sixteen to one for gold, when the open-market ratio of exchange between the two metals had gone to about thirty-two to one against silver, continued to disturb the business of the country until the election of 1896 was taken as indicating that the silver advocates had failed.

After that, there was an opportunity to create intelligently a Gold Standard of the United States; but as usual the nature of any kind of Standard was misconceived, and an awkward, unworkable, statute was enacted. That was the Act of March 14, 1900, the important part of which was as follows: —

The dollar consisting of twenty-five and eight-tenths grains of gold nine-tenths fine shall be the standard unit of value, and all forms of money issued or coined by the United States shall be maintained at a parity of value with this standard, and it shall be the duty of the Secretary of the Treasury to maintain such parity.[16]

Use of the expression "standard unit of value" shows a failure to understand the nature of money, and the technical inaccuracy of this definition of the dollar is to be contrasted with Hamilton's precise statement concerning the money of account of the United States. The statute was grossly defective

[16] R. S. 3511; Sec. 314, Title 31, U. S. Code Annotated.

196

in failing to provide any definite and satisfactory arrangement for buying and selling gold in transactions with other nations. This was the only assurance offered that the paper and silver money of the United States would be able to buy gold. The issuer of a national bank note could pay it with either silver or greenbacks, and the last resort of one who wished to buy gold was the United States Treasury itself. Thus the Government was continued in the humiliating position of being unable to create money without continuing to deal in gold, a duty it should have delegated to some kind of Central Bank.

Soon after enactment of the statute above quoted, there were some amendments of the national bank laws which lowered the requirements for incorporation as a national bank, and also more bonds were made available to secure notes. There was an expansion of bank notes from two hundred and fifty millions to approximately six hundred millions by 1907. In that year there was an overexpansion of contracts to pay money, and a crisis occurred which was to a great extent attributable to inability to obtain money with which to discharge such contracts. That was the case with many sound banks, which would have had little difficulty if there had been a Central Bank, even if it could have done no more than act as a common clearinghouse for the settlement of transactions between banks. The banks, when in different cities, were compelled to use large sums of money in making payments to each other.

After the Panic of 1907, it was easy to foresee the end of what has been called in this chapter the Chase System, for want of a better name. Chase was responsible for it merely to the extent that he permitted it to be started by the Act of Congress authorizing the issue of greenbacks. As a monetary system it was far worse than that of Jackson, and yet better than its successor, the Federal Reserve System. During the period in which the Chase System prevailed there had been introduced into the monetary laws of the United States erroneous and dangerous principles as follows: —

1. For the first time it had been attempted to make money acceptable by declaring it to be legal tender in the payment of private debts.

2. There had been established a new kind of bank to compete with those which already existed, and this set up competition between two branches

of sovercignty in the exercise of control over the business of banking.

3. The Government was made a dealer in the precious metals.

4. Different kinds of money were created, all with varying degrees of desirability.

These defects were in addition to those of the Jacksonian System, which were nearly all continued. During the entire period from 1861 to 1896 there was little certainty as to what kind of money might be used to discharge any contract. There can be no wonder that the history of those years is replete with accounts of financial crises and depressions in business.

4. THE FEDERAL RESERVE SYSTEM

In many respects the financial crisis of 1907 was the most unfortunate in results of any in the long series which the people of the United States have been forced to endure. The need for an emergency supply of currency and central credit assumed such prominence at that time as to result in misleading the authors of the Federal Reserve Act in 1913. Ability of currency to expand was the main feature which attracted their attention, and they mistook that for elasticity. The consequences of this mistake are extremely important, and before considering that Act it is advisable to give a summary of the complicated currency and banking systems of the United States as they were in 1913.

Various laws tampering with the national currency had resulted in there being in circulation in the United States in 1913 the following kinds of money: (1) gold coins, in pieces of two and a half, five, ten and twenty dollars; (2) gold certificates, issued by the United States Treasury as a receipt for the deposit of gold bullion; (3) silver dollars; (4) silver certificates, issued against silver bullion bought at open-market prices under the silver purchase Acts of 1876 and 1890; (5) token coins of less than a dollar; (6) United States notes called "greenbacks"; (7) Treasury notes of 1890; (8) and national bank notes.

The most obvious reform was simplification, to provide for standard gold coins, if they were to be continued, token coins, and only one kind of note. That opportunity was neglected.

In total amount the money was approximately three thousand, four hundred millions at the time the bill to establish the Federal Reserve System was being debated in Congress in the latter part of 1913.

There were nearly seven thousand, five hundred national banks, and several thousand state banks, both of which held total deposits of seventeen thousand million dollars. Currency held by the banks as cash reserves was approximately one half the total stated above. The ability of the banks to expand their deposits, or make contracts to pay money on demand, depended to some extent upon the amount of money available and the use to which it was put. As an illustration, if the banks could be relieved of the burden of carrying one thousand, five hundred million dollars as cash reserves, and that amount released to the public for circulation, the possibilities of credit expansion were enormous.

With eight kinds of currency, when there should have been only three at most, and with competition between two kinds of banks, when there should have been no competition, the Congress proceeded to complicate both by adding two additional kinds of currency and another class of competing banks. The Federal Reserve Act authorized the issuance of Federal Reserve notes and Federal Reserve Bank notes. It also required all national banks to become stockholders (members) of the Reserve Banks, and left that optional with state banks, thus creating two classes of member banks, as well as a class of nonmember banks, all to compete with each other. Consideration should be given to the general nature of the Federal Reserve System, to the banking provisions of the Act, and then to its currency provisions.

The Act divided the United States into twelve districts, for each of which there was established a Federal Reserve Bank. Direct control of these banks was vested in a board of directors for each composed of nine members. Three directors were to be elected by member banks and must "be representative of the stockholding banks," being called Class A. Class B directors were also to be elected by the member banks, but not be officers, directors, or employees of any other bank. Class C directors were three members designated by the Federal Reserve Board and were to be not even stockholders of another bank.

In general the functions of the Reserve Banks were to carry the reserve accounts of member banks; to enable member banks to settle accounts with each other by transfers of credits on the books of their reserve accounts; to obtain the issuance of Federal Reserve notes to be delivered to member banks; to re-discount commercial paper for member banks; and to deal in gold. Member banks were no longer compelled to hold large amounts of cash as reserves. The Reserve Banks were required to maintain reserves in gold "or lawful money" to the extent of thirty-five per cent. of their deposits.

Perhaps the authority of the Reserve Banks to engage in open-market buying and selling of Government bonds deserves special comment. The theory is that when money is too plentiful and business is running into an inflationary boom the System will sell bonds; the purchasers will withdraw money from their banks to pay for them; and the banks will have less money on hand, which will force them to lend less and to call some loans, thus halting the boom. On the other hand, if business is slack the Reserve Banks will buy bonds; the sellers of the bonds will deposit the purchase price received in their banks; the banks will have more money to lend, and that will revive business. This whole manipulative operation ignores the facts that the making of contracts is what gives men employment, and that an employer who has apparatus for the use of which there is no demand has no incentive to borrow money, which is really just a substitute for renting more apparatus. Open-market operations of this kind seem not to have been very successful, which is not surprising, as they substitute a fallacious remedy for the prevention obtainable by the use of correct principles.

The Federal Reserve Board consisted of eight members, two of whom were *ex officio* the Secretary of the Treasury and the Comptroller of the Currency, the other six being appointees of the President of the United States. This Board was to exercise general supervision over the entire system. Among its specifically granted powers of importance were: (1) examination of the condition of Reserve Banks and publication of statements thereof; (2) to permit, and on affirmative vote of five members to require, one Reserve Bank to re-discount for another; (3) to suspend, subject to limitations and taxes, any reserve requirement contained in the Act; (4) to supervise and regulate the issue and retirement of Federal Reserve notes; (5) to review and determine rates of discounts by Federal Reserve Banks.

The statute authorizing the issuance of Federal

Reserve notes is important enough to be quoted in full.

Federal Reserve notes, to be issued at the discretion of the Federal Reserve Board for the purpose of making advances to Federal Reserve banks through the Federal Reserve agents as hereinafter set forth and for no other purpose, are hereby authorized. The said notes shall be obligations of the United States and shall be receivable by all national and member banks and Federal Reserve banks and for all taxes, customs, and other public dues. They shall be redeemed in gold on demand at the Treasury Department of the United States, in the city of Washington, District of Columbia, or in gold or lawful money at any Federal Reserve bank.[17]

It is worthy of notice that this section neither requires the Reserve Banks to sell gold for their notes, as there the notes may "be redeemed . . . in lawful money," nor requires them to buy gold by paying for it in their notes. In fact, there is no provision in the entire Act which compels any part of the Federal Reserve System either to buy gold or to sell it. This omission, as well as the general nature of all the provisions relating to the issuance of notes, indicates that the authors of the Act did not give consideration to the distinctions between the internal

[17] 38 Statutes at Large 265; U.S.C.A. Title 12, Sec. 411.

use of money and the use of gold in commerce with other nations. So far as the purchase of gold is concerned the Act did not make any more definite legal arrangements than those contained in the old laws. True enough the Reserve Banks were authorized to deal in gold, but the point is that they were not *required* by law to buy and sell gold. Certainly the Act was prepared with an erroneous impression as to the nature of the functions of a Central Bank.

The Act contains no limitation whatsoever upon the amount of Federal Reserve notes which may be issued so long as there is maintained a gold reserve worth in dollars forty per cent. of the notes outstanding. When the bill was being debated in the Senate of the United States, Senator Elihu Root pleaded in vain for the adoption of a limitation upon the amount of notes which might be issued similar to those used by Hamilton and in the Bank Charter Act of 1844 for the Bank of England. He pointed out that the effect of the Act would be inflationary, even if not a dollar in currency was added to the then existing total, by releasing for circulation the greater part of nearly one thousand, five hundred million dollars held by the banks as cash reserves, since the legal reserves of banks becoming members of the system were to be transferred to the Reserve Banks. Then, if each dollar's worth of gold that came into the country was to be permitted to increase money by two-and-one-half dollars, and deposits by many times that, he said we might "confidently expect" inflation. As if, on that thirteenth of December, he was peering into the future, with a view of the conditions which would prevail during the great boom and the succeeding depression, he continued: —

This is in no sense a provision for an elastic currency. It does not provide an elastic currency. It provides an expansive currency, but not an elastic one. It provides a currency which may be increased, always increased, but not a currency for which the bill contains any provision compelling reduction. . . .

With the exhaustless reservoir of the Government of the United States furnishing easy money, the sales increase, the businesses enlarge, more new enterprises are started, the spirit of optimism pervades the community. Bankers are not free from it. They are human. The members of the Federal Reserve Board will not be free from it. They are human. Regional Bankers will not be free from it. They are human. All the world moves along on a growing tide of optimism. Everyone is making money. Everyone is growing rich. It goes up and up . . . until finally someone . . . breaks . . . and down comes the whole structure.

I can see in this bill itself, in the discharge of our duty, no influence interposed by us against the occurrence of one of those periods of false and delusive prosperity which inevitably end in ruin and suffering. For the most direful results of the awakening of the people from such a dream are not to be found in the banking houses — no; not even in the business houses. They are to be found among the millions who have lost the means of earning their daily bread.[18]

This prophecy as an unfulfilled one was the subject of ridicule by Senator Carter Glass in his book "An Adventure in Constructive Finance", which was written about 1926.[19] How the prophecy was fulfilled, almost exactly as outlined by Mr. Root, will appear in the next chapter.

The remedy called for by the existing monetary system of the United States in 1913, with respect to the currency, was to create a Fiduciary Issue to replace greenbacks and national bank notes, the approximate amount of which would have been one thousand, two hundred million dollars. That might have been a Government Note Issue, for which the Reserve Banks could have been required to sell gold

---

[18] The whole speech, set out in the *Congressional Record* for Dec. 13, 1913, was a great protest against putting into motion "the Inflationary Process."

[19] See pages 198–202.

at the prevailing statutory price: or such notes might have been a Fiduciary Issue of the Reserve Banks. Any additional notes should have been permitted only for the purpose of buying gold at the rate of a dollar in notes for each dollar's worth of gold, with a requirement that the Reserve Banks sell gold for their notes also, and retire such notes received on a sale of gold. The issuance of gold certificates by the Government should have been discontinued by the substitution of the Reserve Banks for that purpose. Silver certificates probably would have presented a problem of difficulty, but might have been included with the paper currency to be retired by a Fiduciary Issue. The result to be achieved was the use of only one kind of note, or two if the Government was to emit those to be included in a Fiduciary Issue.

It was folly, and reckless disregard of the welfare of the people, to authorize the issuance of more money at a time when arrangements were being made to double the amount in circulation by releasing the cash reserves of the banks. That was so clearly and cogently demonstrated by Mr. Root's speech, referred to above, as to make it difficult to understand why such an able, courageous, and intellectually honest statesman as Senator Carter Glass refused to give heed to the warning. Possibly the explanation is that he relied upon advisers who were economists and did not understand the legal nature of the problem with which they were dealing; whereas Mr. Root's excellent and legally trained mind had a deep appreciation of the work of Alexander Hamilton, an equally great lawyer, to whose example Mr. Root appealed eloquently and convincingly, but in vain. Whatever the explanation, the fact is that, after Great Britain had learned that the gold reserve principle would not work and had in 1844 abandoned it for that of Alexander Hamilton, which she demonstrated again would work successfully, the Congress of the United States was persuaded to revert to the gold-reserve principle. By authorizing the Federal Reserve Banks to issue two dollars and a half in money for each dollar's worth of gold they acquired, the Act made the foundation for all contracts to pay money in the United States a speculative margin of forty per cent.

With respect to changes in the banking system which might have been made by the Act, there was neglected the opportunity to provide that no bank, not a member of the Federal Reserve System, should be permitted to make a contract to pay money on demand. Then all banks which were to engage in the business of making such contracts should have been compelled to be of one kind, either state or national. It must be recognized, however, that political conditions, and the prevalence of erroneous theories as to the application of the Constitution to laws relating to money and banking, made a correct and thorough reform impossible.

Except that there was provision for the keeping of banking reserves, and that it was made easier to finance a war, the Federal Reserve System retained most of the defects of the Chase System, and added some of its own.

CHAPTER VI

MISMANAGEMENT

ALTHOUGH during the period from 1914 to 1933 there was no important legislation, in the United States, which directly affected money and banking, some of the acts of the Government during that time were of great importance so far as the monetary process as a whole was concerned. In fact, the depression which began in 1929 is as much attributable to the actions of the Government of the United States as was that of 1837. The great difference was that in the latter case the power of the Government was greater, the scope of its application wider, and the results of its use more severe. More than mere money and banking now becomes involved. The monetary process touches everything, and is reacted upon by almost every event.

It is necessary to emphasize again that the first and greatest of the three instruments used to carry on the monetary process is a contract. Money and banks are national instruments; but contracts may be begun in one nation and consummated in another. Therefore, the monetary process has its international aspects as well as its national. If the making, or performance, of contracts is restrained in one place, there will be set up a restraint in another place; and if there are restrictions imposed upon the making of one kind of contracts men will also be prevented from entering into other kinds. During the period under consideration, the power of the United States was first used to cause a great expansion of contracts to pay money; and then it was applied to restrict the making of contracts to exchange goods, on the performance of which the contracts to pay money depended for their discharge.

Consequently, a correct appraisal of the facts must involve looking beyond the monetary and banking disturbances in the United States, which were not so much causes as symptoms. There must be taken into consideration some events which may at first seem to have only a remote connection with monetary affairs, but which were directly related to the process as a whole.

After the termination of the World War, the only

possibility of a Standard of International Trade was one in which the dollar would be the principal monetary unit. Also the only possibility of a performance of those duties in international affairs which naturally fall to the lot of the leading nation was that the United States would assume them. The power of Great Britain, as has been said before, was decreased too much by the war to justify her in continuing to run the risks of either rôle. The situation is to be considered in two aspects: first, that of the Standard; and, second, that of the leading nation's rôle. With reference to both there was a peculiarly unfortunate combination of circumstances.

As to the Standard of International Trade, the world seemed not to appreciate the fact that the nature of the Standard had changed. Constant discussion of *the* Gold Standard may have been responsible for the general failure to make allowance for the difference between *a* gold standard created and managed by Great Britain under good laws, and a gold standard created and managed by the United States under bad laws. The dollar was on a gold standard, and that seems to have misled the financial interests of the world into assuming that they might rely upon the continued operation of *the* Gold Standard.

In many respects the situation at the end of the war is comparable to that which existed at the end of the Napoleonic Wars. There were two great differences, however. First, at the end of the Napoleonic Wars all the great nations were equally exhausted, or at least Great Britain was not so much exhausted in comparison with the others that she was prevented from taking up the duties of a kind of international arbiter to try to lead the way back to peace and prosperity. There was no outside nation as a rival not damaged by the wars. Of course, Great Britain had not played any such leading rôle before the Napoleonic Wars as she came to play later. But in 1918 the United States was much richer and more powerful, in comparison with other nations, than she was prior to the war. Thus the position of leadership was then shifted to an environment and influences which were completely different from any that had ever before affected the actions of the leading nation. Second, prior to the Napoleonic Wars there had been no real International Standard of Trade. The British Gold Standard was then still indefinite, and had not worked itself up to such a pre-eminent position that the other nations had been compelled to try to follow it. Consequently, the efforts which Great Britain made from 1816 to 1846 to establish a successful International Standard were contributions tending all the time to improve the situation. It may be said that after the Napoleonic Wars there was a change from no Standard to, first, a Standard of limited extent, and, later, to a good Standard generally accepted. But after the War of 1914 there was a change from a good and successful Standard to a poor and unsuccessful one.

Therefore, it becomes necessary to show in more detail why the Gold Standard of the United States was a bad one. This will be attempted by testing it according to the principles applicable to the most powerful nation which were stated in the latter part of the fourth chapter. The period under discussion is from November 11, 1918, to March 4, 1933.

I. There was to some extent a free and open market for gold in the United States, but the laws provided for it very awkwardly, and by their very nature gave a threat that in a time of crisis there would not be gold for sale. The subject of the free sale of gold is considered here, and that of a market where it is certain that gold will be bought is discussed later.

What ultimate and positive assurance was there that anyone who desired to buy gold in the United States would be able to do so? No bank was compelled by law to sell gold, although it was generally customary for them to do so. All contracts of the banks to pay money on demand were, according to the law of legal tender, dischargeable by the offer of "lawful" money. Such money might be greenbacks, or various kinds of *promises* to deliver gold, to such extent that, strictly speaking, there was no certainty that gold could be obtained outside of the Treasury of the United States. Consequently, the position of the Treasury must be considered.

The so-called Gold Standard Act made it the duty of the Secretary of the Treasury to "maintain at a parity" with 23.22 grains of pure gold all kinds of money of the United States. The greater part of the gold which the Treasury held was specifically pledged for delivery against gold certificates, which were generally regarded as warehouse receipts. Such gold was not a reserve for sale in exchange for the other kinds of money. The rather indirect requirement of the law that gold be available for sale for the other kinds of money applied to: greenbacks, in excess of three hundred million dollars; National Bank notes, in excess of seven hundred millions; and Federal Reserve notes, usually in excess of three thousand millions. It is to be noted that Federal Reserve notes were by statute expressly made obligations of the United States, redeemable in gold at the Treasury. Thus without counting silver certificates and subsidiary coins, which would add several hundred millions more, the Treasury was obligated to sell gold to an amount in excess of four thousand millions. Against that liability, excluding the gold specifically pledged against certificates, there was usually on hand *in the Treasury,* somewhat less than two hundred millions in gold, although the Federal Reserve Banks held large stocks.

These awkward statutory requirements constituted a serious threat to the existence of a free and open gold market. With such a threat hanging over it in a time of crisis the market could not be free from one of the most destructive restrictions which could be placed upon it — fear.

II. That there was not a free and open market for goods in the United States needs no demonstration. The restrictions imposed upon the market for goods by the Tariff Act of 1922 were the most severe on record up until that time, and the Act of 1930 imposed even greater restrictions. Further comment on this subject must be deferred.

III. Successful application of the third principle of the laws of the leading nation, which relate to the monetary process, depends to a great extent upon the correct use of Government credit in creating money. That principle requires money, which will always be able to buy gold at the price fixed, and cannot, on account of gold, be either excessively created or contracted in amount.

The Bill which became the Federal Reserve Act was prepared upon the mistaken theory that the possession of one dollar's worth of gold could be used as the means of creating two dollars and a half in paper. It was an observation of William Graham Sumner that this mistaken belief has always been the curse of monetary legislation in the United States. All attempts to make use of this erroneous principle must be bolstered up by an abuse of Government credit.

The Federal Reserve Act used Government credit to support Federal Reserve notes in two respects. First, they were made receivable in all payments to the Government; second, they were made "obligations of the United States." The first alone, under the circumstances, would have been too much. There had already been created upon Government credit, and outstanding at the time the Act was passed, about one thousand, five hundred million dollars — consisting of national bank notes, greenbacks, subsidiary coins, silver dollars, and silver certificates. The Act extended this use of Government credit to the support of an unprecedented speculation in gold as a means of creating money.

Correct application of this third principle also requires that there be a distinction between contracts to pay money, which are internal, and contracts to deliver gold, which are international. The great defect of the Federal Reserve Act, in this respect, was that it provided for an unlimited expansion of contracts to pay money. It is obvious that the more money there is the more such contracts can be made after business goes into a boom. Then the overexpansion, once allowed to exist without regard to its cause, must be supported by the ability to maintain in existence at least the same amount of money. By permitting the creation of "easy money" the Federal Reserve Act presented the danger that an enlarged superstructure of credit, consisting of thousands of contracts to pay money, might be demolished by the loss of gold contracting the "base" support. Therefore, the Federal Reserve System, in a time of crisis, would have to give more attention to maintaining a supply of gold large enough to support its internal credit structure, instead of going to the aid of weak nations whose currencies needed gold in order to continue to exist on reasonable conditions. This prevented the system from being able to perform successfully, as the agent of the United States Government, its duties as manager of an International Standard. For, if it could not perform its functions in a crisis, the System would do more harm than good. The laws permitted, and encouraged, the use of gold in such unwise ways and then imposed such restrictions upon its removal from the improper use of creating internal inflation to the proper one of making foreign payments that the System was compelled to have a tremendous stock of gold in order to have any "free" for sale in commerce with other nations. In normal times, the System could, and did, aid in the distribution of gold to other nations, but in a time of crisis the very law to which the System owned its existence made it worse than useless. How such a crisis came about, and the disastrous effects of the Act here criticized, will be related further on in this chapter.

IV. There is some exaggeration involved in calling the Federal Reserve System, or any one of the Federal Reserve Banks, a Central Bank. The authors of the Act concentrated their attention upon creating a source of supply for "emergency currency", and placed all their emphasis upon the internal functions of the System with very little regard for those functions which a Central Bank is supposed to perform for commerce with other nations. This is well illustrated by the failure to require in the Act that the Federal Reserve Banks buy gold. Actually there was very little need for such a provision, but theoretically the Act placed too much reliance upon the fact that everyone generally wishes to acquire gold. Of course, there were the provisions for free coinage of gold and its deposit with the Treasury in exchange for gold certificates, but both should have been repealed. For these provisions there should have been substituted the requirement that the Federal Reserve Banks buy all gold offered them, either by giving for it a credit on their books or by issuing notes. Had this been done, and a Fiduciary Issue with a limitation created, the System would have been able to act as a public merchant in buying and selling gold, and it would have had more direct control over the currency.

So far as the keeping of reserve accounts was concerned, there can be very little criticism of the Act. But the requirement that a reserve of thirty-five per cent. in either gold or "lawful money" be maintained against the reserve accounts of the member banks was a clear failure to distinguish between the internal circulation of money and the external circulation of the precious metals. Furthermore, once a great inflation was permitted, this requirement as to gold served to some extent to tie the hands of the System with respect to keeping gold "free" for sale.

V. The requirement that there be a good system of banks for keeping checking accounts applies with peculiar force to the leading nation. The contracts to pay money on demand made by these banks must be unquestionable, or hoarding of gold will result. In a crisis of international scope, the banks of the leading nation are not supposed to be a source of demand for gold. Here was a feature in which the Federal Reserve Act was especially bad.

National banks had been established as a means of financing a war. Even at the time of the Civil War, it had been recognized that there should not be two competing systems of banks, and an abortive attempt to prevent the existence of banks chartered by the states had been made by forbidding them to issue bank notes. [When that failed, the National Government continued to intermeddle in a field from which it should have withdrawn or over which it should have assumed exclusive jurisdiction. As to that, however, there was a grave constitutional question. Had the National Government power to forbid banks chartered by the states to make contracts to pay money on demand and to perform those contracts by means of checks? Historically, the Administration which went into office in 1913 was committed to the principle that the National Government had not that power. Therefore, instead of attempting to use such power, which it clearly had, to bring about unification of banking into one system, there was an effort to persuade state banks to become members of the Federal Reserve System. It would have been far better to abolish the existing national banks and make all member banks state banks with a Central Bank at their head. The proper kind of requirements for membership could have been imposed, and member banks, as well as the Reserve Banks, could have been forbidden to lend to nonmember banks. But the Act left the banking system of the country to consist of thousands of independent banks, without the unified general control of a Central Bank.

The great effect of this lack of unity was competition in making liberal laws. One instance of this is to be found in an amendment to the Federal Reserve Act permitting national banks to act as administrators and executors of the estates of deceased persons. The National Government has no power over the appointment of either, and the appointment must be under state law. Some of the states then passed laws forbidding national banks to be appointed by their courts to perform such functions, and the Supreme Court of the United States decided that despite such a state law a national bank could act as executor.[1] Here was the worst possible confusion

[1] This is a typical instance of erroneous and confusing intermeddling by the National Government with local affairs of the states, over which they were intended to have, and should have, exclusive control. The statute — U.S.C.A. Title 12, Sec. 248 (K) — empowers the Federal Reserve Board to permit national banks to act as trustees, executors, administrators, and guardians

of legislative powers. This competition in lawmaking between forty-eight states on one side and the National Government on the other tended to prevent the development of a good system of banks. Although it cannot be regarded as the cause of so many bank failures during the years from 1929 to 1933, the weakness of the system was contributed to by this competition in liberalizing bank charters. Clearly the principle which should have been adopted with respect to this question of constitutional power over banking was to put in the Federal Reserve Act a well-defined dividing line between the powers of the states and those of the National Government so that each would have remained in its own field.

Thus, at the time the United States was called upon to play the rôle of leading nation, and to assume the duties of establishing and administering a Standard of International Trade, her monetary laws did not fully comply with any one of the essential prin-

---

of estates. The effect of the statute, Burnes National Bank *v.* Duncan, 265 U. S. 19, is that if the law of a state permits a state bank to serve in such capacities then a national bank must be permitted to do so even if specifically forbidden by a statute of the state. This takes away from a state the control of its own courts, and goes far beyond any exercise of national power contemplated by the most extreme Federalist of Hamilton's time.

ciples, most of which had been completely violated. Under the laws by which it was created, there was little hope that the dollar could serve as a monetary unit upon which to base international payments. This should have been apparent to the responsible officials of the Government of the United States, but there was a dearth of statesmanship.

Having reviewed some of the disadvantages which the monetary laws of the country imposed upon management of the International Standard, attention should now be given the unfortunate aspects of the position of the United States in world affairs. Although it is commonly said that the people of this nation were not accustomed to taking an interest in foreign affairs, it is doubtful whether that view is strictly accurate. The Monroe Doctrine and several disputes on its account, the Spanish War, and the intermeddling in Mexico all show that there was concern with the affairs of other nations when these were considered to be of interest to the people of the United States. The aversion was to becoming entangled with the affairs of nations with which we had no direct interest, and that generally confined our participation in international affairs to the Western Hemisphere. The war on the Barbary pirates and President Roosevelt's action about the Perdicaris incident in Morocco tend to show that interest in affairs not strictly American, geographically, could be aroused. There was no prejudice against taking action, so far as European affairs were concerned, purely because they were European; the very fact that we went into the World War is proof of that. If there was an interest in European affairs, a direct concern with them, then the attitude was to attend to it. The Administration in power at the time of the war's termination was responsible for arousing a prejudice against any kind of participation in the affairs of European nations. That was done with the best of intentions, but the result has been to give an otherwise impossible strength to strict nationalism and isolationists.

Instead of devoting its efforts to making a treaty of peace which would definitely terminate the war, the Peace Conference was persuaded by President Wilson to divert its attention to the preparation of an international agreement designed to prevent wars in the future. There was thus, in the very beginning of the period under consideration, a tendency on the part of the United States to substitute the action of a group of nations for its own performance of the duties of leadership. The disposition was to assume that the League of Nations would manage, and to rely upon that without attempting to obtain for the United States more power over the League's management than a mere vote would give. A demand for more would, of course, have been contrary to the whole spirit of the League. But the fallacy of the idea of the League was the proposal to tie the hands of the most powerful nation, the one upon which the duty of leadership was inevitably cast, and to make it act in concert with the weaker nations, according to their votes. It was the restriction in that respect, the agreement to act in international affairs according to the desires of a majority of other nations, which caused the people of the United States to reject the Treaty of Versailles.

The mistake in provoking a bitter political fight over ratification of the Treaty prevented any later appeal to the people of the United States to be reasonable in their attitude toward Europe. Prejudices and hatreds against Europe aroused in the struggle about the League of Nations placed the Government at a disadvantage. Had there been an effort to develop gradually a public sentiment which would have enabled the United States to make a beginning in assuming the rôle of leading nation, both the war debts and the tariff would have been dealt with more intelligently. The result of the impractical idealism which sought to persuade the most powerful nation to bind itself to act in agreement with other nations was to substitute a selfish attitude for consideration of duties and responsibilities.

In turning to consideration of events, it must be admitted that the Federal Reserve System was of great aid in financing the war. There would have been, necessarily, some inflation at the end of the war, although there was entirely too much, and deflation came in 1921. The national debt, however, was not large in comparison with the natural wealth of the country, hardly reaching ten per cent. of the national wealth. In 1921 there was full opportunity for the United States to take the right road. When the Harding Administration came into office in that year, it was less than eight years since Senator Root had so well pointed out the defects in the Federal Reserve Act, and it must be remembered that he had had the support of the conservatives in opposing the Act's passage without his amendments to limit its inflationary possibilities. The Republicans could easily have pointed to the Depression of 1921 as a result of the Act to a great extent, and passed amendments along the lines originally proposed. They neglected that opportunity, however, for one to raise the tariff. Thus they added to the dangers of inflation those of a restrictive and destructive force.

For a while the dollar had to serve as the monetary unit of an International Standard, as the pound sterling was fluctuating without a fixed price for gold. That condition continued until 1925, when the pound sterling was restored to par. After that, there was apparently a Standard for commerce among nations; but actually there was not one. The United States would not assume the burden of making the Standard continue to work in a time of crisis, and Great Britain could not do so. It seems hardly accurate to say that there was a struggle for ascendancy between the dollar and the pound. Actually there was some co-operation between the monetary authorities of the two nations, but co-operation of that kind cannot ever establish a Standard which will continue to exist through a crisis. To the extent that there was competition between the two currency units there was no Standard. Many people, however, were deceived into believing that a weight of gold was the Standard. The situation was that the dollar could be bought with goods only under difficulties, and the ability of the pound sterling to buy gold at the price fixed was being maintained precariously. Each was lacking in the characteristics required of a monetary unit to be used in the administration of an International Standard, and there was completely lacking any unified control by the monetary authorities of either nation. If there was a Standard, there was no hope that it could survive a crisis.

The inflation which prevailed in the United States from 1922 to 1929 was of a peculiar kind, but the most subtle and dangerous that can occur — a gold inflation in the most powerful nation. Experiences with that kind of inflation in Great Britain during the decade preceding the Bank Charter Act of 1844 tend to support this view. The monetary gold stocks of the United States increased from around twelve hundred million dollars' worth in 1914 to more than double that in 1920, and to about four thousand millions in 1925. That was enough gold, on the gold "base" or reserve theory of the Federal Reserve Act, to support the circulation of ten thousand million dollars. Money in active circulation rose from about seventeen hundred millions in 1913 to more than four thousand millions in 1920, and was at about the same figure in 1925. Demand deposits had more than doubled from 1914 to 1920, and then went up by six thousand millions more to twenty-six thousand in 1925. During the period 1914–1920, in which money had been multiplied by nearly two and a half and demand deposits by two, the country had consumed an appreciable percentage of its real wealth in the war. Actually the nation was no richer in real national wealth in 1920 than it was in 1914. The gold which had come in was an accidental accumulation of an oversupply of one commodity, and it was neither any increase in real wealth nor a proper means of creating more money.

Other nations had been unable to go back on a gold standard, and owners of gold had little desire to sell it to the Central Banks of those nations when there was the probability that, if it should become necessary to repurchase it, a higher price would have to be paid. Also the Central Banks of those nations were, for a while, unwilling to buy gold with the possibility of later being required by law to sell it at a lower price. Consequently, the owners of gold sought to sell it for money with which they could buy it back at the same price, and the gold thus came to the United States. Its presence was purely accidental, and it was bad enough to permit each 23.22 grains so acquired to expand money by one dollar, to say nothing of allowing the reserve principle to increase money at a greater rate. If there had been prescribed during this time a limited Fiduciary Issue, and no money of any kind resting upon public credit, it would have been a mistake to have outstanding a single dollar of the Fiduciary Issue. This gold inflation was very deceptive, however, and after the Depression of 1921 terminated it was allowed to proceed at a greater pace.

The fact that the laws treated gold as the one safe method of creating money at a liberal rate, instead of as a commodity to be used in commerce with other nations, was a great force in causing the general attitude of the public to be in favor of all measures which would not only enable the United States to keep the gold it had, but help it to obtain more. This belief in the power of gold to create money in the proportion of two-and-one-half to one was in some measure responsible for both the high-tariff policies and those with regard to the war debts. There was an *apparent* benefit in both the tariff and the war debt payments, in that they tended to increase the hoard of gold. Had there been a legal limit upon the use of gold as an automatic creator of money, the public would not have been so easily misled into regarding it as an increase in real wealth. This prejudice, or survival of beliefs based upon the prevalence of barter, which had become erroneous with the use of internal contracts to pay money, joined the prejudice against Europe to sustain high tariffs and cause demand for payment of the war debts in gold.

The presence of the great quantities of gold made it very easy to make, and for a while to perform, contracts to pay money. The extent of inflation is not to be measured by the total sum of money in circulation and contracts of the banks to pay money on demand. Some account must be taken of the numerous other contracts to pay money which were not subject to demand — such as savings accounts; corporate, state, and municipal bonds; mortgages, and all kinds of indebtedness. All these expanded greatly, and could not have done so to such an excess but for the presence of the gold and the knowledge that it *could* be used under the liberal terms of the Federal Reserve Act to create more money. The very presence of the gold created, in bankers and business men, a tendency to be free in making contracts to pay money. Brokers' loans never could have reached the stupendous sum of eight thousand million dollars had the Federal Reserve Act been revised to be a proper monetary law for the most powerful nation. It is to be noted that the authors of the Act are not alone to blame in this respect. At the time they were writing the law, the United States was *not* the most powerful nation. Also, the tariff was not so excessively high, and they expected it to be reduced, which was done. When their Administration went out of office the tariff was reasonable, and the Harding Administration made three mistakes: raising the tariff, failing to amend the Federal Reserve Act, and, at the same time, requiring the war debts to be paid in gold. The tariff, the war debts, and the change in the international position of the United States made amendments to the Federal Reserve Act imperative.

As the nations of Europe went on a gold standard, they seem to have thought that they were returning to the old Gold Standard, and to have assumed that the United States would let some of its gold flow to them. For a while there was an inclina-

tion on the part of both bankers and the Federal
Reserve Board to let some of the gold go. The
bankers made large foreign loans which tended to
redistribute gold to other nations. That was inter-
rupted, however, in 1928, when the inflationary
speculation in stocks in the United States began to
draw gold back to New York on account of high
interest rates. But that, with intelligent policies on
the part of the United States Government, would
have been a temporary interruption only. At the
time, the United States was just beginning to be
called upon to play the rôle of Administrator of the
International Standard. The European nations had
not been trying to follow, or use, the Standard for
long. Until that time nothing had happened either
to impair permanently the ability of the Standard
to work, or perhaps even to warn that it was not
likely to work.

A warning was not long in coming, however. In
the fall of 1929, the Stock Market in New York began to give indications that the financial inflation
in the United States had passed its peak. At the
time, the Congress had been wrangling for months
over a bill to raise the tariff, and threatening the
business of the world with the most foolish and dam-

aging action possible under the circumstances. There was a warning, to which the President of the United States should have given heed by announcing to the Congress that this was no time to raise the tariff and that he would veto any bill to that effect. The Congress continued on its evil work, however, and passed the bill in June 1930. Approval of the bill by the President made clear to all the world that the United States from that time on would make little effort to perform the duties of the most powerful nation. It is doubtful whether any chief executive officer of a government of a modern civilized nation has ever made a more unfortunate mistake. The bill had barely passed the Senate by a vote of forty-two to forty, and there was no chance to pass it over a veto. More than one thousand of the leading economists of the country made a plea to the President to veto the bill, and pointed out clearly why it should be vetoed.

The Tariff Act of 1930 was the first unmistakable indication that the United States would restrain commerce among nations instead of promoting it. The Act of 1922 had come a little too soon in the period of changed international relations to give any such positive indication. Moreover, the war debt payments had hardly commenced then, and the other nations were not then making determined efforts to obtain gold with which to support their currencies. Also it is to be remembered that, although foreign lending had declined greatly in 1928, it was not definitely terminated prior to June of 1930. Until that time there was hope that it might be resumed on a conservative basis, so that gold could be more reasonably distributed. Then it was that the other nations needed gold for the support of their currencies.

There is here, again, danger of overestimating the importance of both gold and money. Primarily what began to afflict the nations of the world in 1930 was not a lack of gold, or rather a corner of gold by the United States, although that did have some effect. The most important factor was the restraint placed by the United States upon the making and performance of contracts. That restraint was applied both outside the United States and in it. An inquiry into the manner and results of its application should begin with contracts outside the United States.

So far as the nations of the world had returned to a gold standard, — and the more important ones had, — the prevailing legal system was such that contracts to pay money *might* be required to be discharged by delivery of gold, but were *expected* to be discharged by the substitution of a third person's promise to pay either money, if the contract was internal, or gold, if the contract was one of commerce among nations. The contracts which could be substituted for another contract to pay money arose almost exclusively out of the exchange of goods. If the quantities of goods being exchanged decreased, then the number of contracts available for offsetting promises, either to pay money or deliver gold, became less; and there was more and more the probability of having to make actual deliveries of gold on external contracts and of money on internal contracts. It required no great number of actual performances of contracts to deliver gold for payments to another country to cause a perceptible decrease in the supply of gold held by any one of the secondary nations. That, in itself, was sufficient to cause a reluctance to make contracts either to pay money or to deliver gold. Under the British Administration of the International Standard there had always been in London a free market for both goods and gold, plus a disposition to relieve a situation of this kind by sending gold to the country so affected. Under the leadership of the United States, however, there was really no one of the three. Theoretically there was a free gold market, but it was impossible to get goods in over the high tariff wall for the purpose of buying the gold, and there was no other way to get it. Also, any disposition on the part of the United States to relieve most foreign nations from such pressure was effectively prevented by the fact that gold had to be shipped from the country affected in order to meet war debt payments. For a little more than a year after the Tariff Act of 1930 went into effect, Great Britain relieved the situation somewhat by maintaining, at a loss to herself, a free market for both goods and gold. This offered some opportunity to other nations to sell their goods in London in order to get the gold which they could not obtain in New York, as well as that which they had to send there for war debt payments. Great Britain, under such circumstances, could not continue to sell gold at a fixed price or to maintain a free and open market for goods. She was compelled to abandon both in 1931. That left the other nations with no market place in which they could sell goods freely for gold.

Perhaps it would have been better if all nations other than France and the United States had stopped with an abandonment of selling gold at a fixed price, without trying to prevent their citizens from making contracts with those of other nations to send out gold in exchange for goods. But each nation desired, not only to retain the gold which it had, but to get more. All began to place restrictions upon the making of contracts by raising tariff barriers against goods coming in from other countries. Most of them went further, and forbade the export of gold. In comparison with the restrictions placed upon the making of contracts, the increased demand for gold was of minor consequence. It is customary to place a great deal of emphasis upon the fact that the price level was falling all the time. That, however, was more of a consequence of restrictive laws preventing the making and performance of contracts than it was a cause of the general stagnation of business. Business men who were not free to make contracts could not continue to pay the men whom they had formerly employed to perform their contracts. The restrictions imposed by law, which in many countries came near to being a complete abolition of freedom of contract, caused unemployment as the result of there being no contracts to perform. With men prevented by law from making contracts, the world's gold supply might have been doubled, or trebled, and there would still have been unemployment as well as falling prices.

The power of the United States was used to restrain commerce among nations. It has, ever since June 17, 1930, been to business men all over the world a constant threat of the application of all the resources of the most powerful nation to prevent the performance of any contract into which they might enter. No one has known, or dared try to guess, what the next foolish and destructive use of the power of the United States might be. There could be no hope that a nation with such a Government could escape paying for its own folly. It had prevented the making and performance of contracts not only by citizens of other nations but by its own citizens as well.

In considering the internal situation in the United States during the period from 1929 to 1935, it is necessary to keep in mind the cumulative effects of the Federal Reserve Act, the tariff, and the war debts, as the chief destructive factors created by law. The first of these created inflation, and the second

243

and third made it certain that the collapse of the inflation would be even more violent than usual. In addition, the generally defective banking laws denied unity and strength to the banking system as a whole.

Many have considered that one of the great causes of the severity of the latest depression in the United States was the great inequality between prosperity on the farm and in the financial and industrial centers. It may be well worth while to pause here to inquire into the nature of the agricultural depression. It is to be remembered that the farmers did not really emerge from the Depression of 1921. Also, in times of great economic hardship the favorite remedy of the farmers has been more money — inflation. In this respect they seem to have chosen a policy of which they have been the chief victims. The inflation which occurred from 1922 to 1929 was largely a financial one, partly industrial, and certainly did not reach the farms. As to those products of agriculture which are not exported in great quantities, the capacity of the country to consume them being limited, an inflationary boom can do little to increase their price. Agricultural products of the kinds of which there is a large surplus for export have a world price largely, which is in gold. Inflation on a "gold base", with a fixed price for gold, cannot serve to raise those prices, as the farmer, indirectly, exchanges his exported products for gold, which he sells for dollars. If there is internal inflation of other prices, — as there was during that period, — the dollars which he receives are worth much less than they would be if the "gold base" reserve theory had never been adopted. In other words, the Federal Reserve Act, by inflating the prices of things which the farmer bought when it could not inflate the prices of things he had to sell, was the first cause of the farmer having no share in whatever kind of prosperity there was from 1922 to 1929.

The tariff added to the burdens of the farmer. There was no justice in preventing the exchange of agricultural products for the things which the farmer needed. This restriction upon the farmer's freedom of contract was what destroyed the market for him, and was to a great extent responsible for the severity of the depression in the United States. What happened was that the intermediaries who completed the export transactions for farmers, and acquired gold in a foreign market, were not allowed to use the gold in that market to buy cheap goods for the farmer, as they could not get the goods into the United States without paying a prohibitive tax. The consequence of their being forced to take away from those markets all gold received for the farm products of the United States was that there was less and less gold in the markets, until finally there was none to bring out.

When the farmers were prevented by law from making contracts by which they could sell their produce, no one could expect them to perform the contracts which they had made to pay money to others. Thousands of banks in the agricultural sections of the country held contracts to pay money made by farmers. Also those banks had made thousands of contracts to pay money on demand. As the farmers became unable to perform their contracts the banks could not perform theirs. A wave of bank failures went over the agricultural regions, and that began to spread doubt as to the ability of banks in general to perform their contracts to pay money on demand.

The restrictive effects of the tariff were not confined to the farmers. Many manufacturers also became unable to make contracts to sell their products in foreign markets, and as they had fewer contracts naturally they had to reduce the number of men who were employed for the sole purpose of enabling their employers to perform contracts. Also the inability of the farmers to sell their products removed them from the market as an effective source of demand for many of the products of domestic manufacturers. This spreading of the inability to make contracts was the great source of disturbance. It seems to have been a cause, rather than a result, of the falling price level. As the manufacturers decreased the number of their employees, the ability of those men, who were without contracts of employment, to perform their contracts to pay money, — on mortgages on their homes, small loans at the banks, debts to their merchants and of other personal kinds, — resulted in the forced sale of many kinds of property pledged, or seized by process of law, for the performance of those contracts. Is not the paradox of want in the midst of a great plentifulness of natural resources to be explained by the restrictions placed upon the making of contracts? The only method of distribution available had to begin with the making of contracts, and for its success was dependent upon freedom of contract, which a foolish government denied.

People began to feel that they preferred to run the risk of keeping money itself to giving it to a bank in exchange for its contract to pay an equivalent sum on demand. Then they demanded that the banks perform entirely too many of their contracts to pay money on demand, and the banks had to have more and more money with which to meet their contracts. That brought about a great increase in the amount of currency in circulation, which makes it necessary to turn to the Federal Reserve Act again.

The United States had been increasing its supply of gold for about a year in the fall of 1931. The supply then reached the great total of five thousand million dollars' worth, of which the Federal Reserve System held some three thousand millions. As the loss of confidence in the ability of the member banks to perform their contracts to pay on demand caused a necessary expansion in the amount of currency available, the only way to meet the requirement was through the issuance of Federal Reserve notes. But at the same time that the Federal Reserve System was forced to expand its note issue, it began to lose gold, and, as Federal Reserve notes increased, the limit of the forty per cent. gold reserve was brought nearer and nearer by decreases in the amount of gold which constituted that reserve.

It is important to note here how the use of the gold on hand was restricted by law so that the crisis was made worse. The gold held by the Government was mostly pledged against gold certificates, and these could not be increased except by the acquisition of more gold. Gold, gold coins, and gold certificates were being hoarded to a great extent. A part of the gold held by the Reserve System was tied up in its requirement of a reserve against its deposits. As to that reserve, which had to be thirty-five per cent. of the amount of deposits, either in gold or "lawful money", there was almost as much demand for the "lawful money" as for the gold, and it was a useless provision.

The simultaneous increase in Federal Reserve Bank notes and decrease in the supply of the gold upon which, under the erroneous principle of the law, they were "based", continued until in the early part of 1932 the System found itself with only a few hundred million dollars' worth of "free gold", — that is to say, gold which was not required as a reserve against either notes outstanding or deposits of member banks. Here was the very crisis which

Senator Root had predicted when he made his speech proposing amendments to the bill in 1913. The millions who "had lost the means of earning their daily bread" had long been a sad fulfillment of his prophecy. This crisis was met temporarily by an Act of Congress which permitted Government bonds to be used as security for Federal Reserve notes. It was the same old story of a crisis occurring as the result of improper legislation, and some more legislation of the same kind being enacted to meet it. Enough gold was made free, however, by this new provision to enable the demands for gold to be met temporarily.

The Government was unable to understand that its own restraint upon commerce among nations was the primary cause of the stagnation in business. World commerce had decreased by nearly sixty per cent. In great part that was attributable to the failure of the United States to perform its duties as the most powerful nation. Instead of trying to free the markets of the world, it imposed a restraining power upon them. Its tariff policies had brought on tariff wars and restrictions on trade all over the world. The clear duty of the Government of the United States was to prevent the existence of such restrictions, but instead of doing that it led the way in imposing them.

After the crisis which came very near to forcing the United States in the first part of 1932 to abandon the Standard of International Trade which it had been supposed to administer, the downward trend of business continued. Having cornered the gold market and created large sums of paper money on that, the Government could not provide a remedy by authorizing the creation of more paper money upon its own bonds.

The banking system of the nation was essentially weak; not from any fault of bankers, except to the extent that they, like all others, had been deceived into following the inflationary lead of the laws, but because men in general had been first persuaded by the inflationary process to make too many contracts and then restricted in their ability to perform them. The banks were the ultimate victims of the Government's restriction upon the enterprise of its citizens. There were restrictions other than the tariff, but they were not so directly related to the monetary process.

The final breakdown of the organization of money and banking built around the Federal Reserve System came just as a new Administration was taking control of the Government of the United States. Too much doubt about the ability of the banks to perform their contracts came to be expressed in widespread demand that a great part of them be performed at once. There was not enough money for that, as it had never been intended that there should be. The disposition of the Government, however, to do nothing except create more money, showed that it was likely that so much money would be created as to make it unable to buy gold. Therefore, it was but a short step from demanding that the banks perform their contracts to pay money on demand by delivering money to demanding that the Government comply with its guaranty that all the money would buy gold at the price of 23.22 grains pure to the dollar.

Thus the government of a powerful and wealthy nation finally became the victim of its own folly; its policy of restriction became so universal in its application that that government itself was forced into the humiliating position of refusing to perform its own contracts.

Is it fair to say that the organization for conducting the monetary process in the United States which was established under the leadership of the Federal Reserve System was worse than the one which it superseded? It seems so. The System was responsible for the erection of a speculative pyramid of contracts to pay money which could not be supported over a period of years unless those years were abnormally good ones. There was no incentive supplied by the laws under which the System operated to bring about a gradual contraction of the war inflation. Justice to the authors of the Act, however, demands that it be said that they did not expect the System to be operated in accompaniment to any such policies of government as were pursued from 1921 to 1933. That the Act itself caused an inflation from which of necessity there would have been a severe reaction may hardly be denied. It promoted the making of contracts to pay money to an extent which could not be supported under any circumstances reasonably to be expected. The unnecessary extremes to which the reaction from the inflation went are not attributable to the System, but rather to the restrictions upon the making of contracts which resulted from the failure of the United States even to attempt to perform its duties as a leader of nations, and from its tariff and war debt policies.

CHAPTER VII

DESTRUCTION OF MONETARY STANDARDS

CONSIDERATION of monetary legislation in the United States since March 4, 1933, presents many difficulties. There must be kept in view not only the principles applicable to designation and regulation of the functions of the instruments used in the monetary process, but the principles to be deduced from the Constitution. As to the latter, the decisions of the Supreme Court in the "Gold Clause Cases" have sustained the validity of some of the legislation, but have not given clear directions for the trend which future enactments should follow — which indeed is beyond the duties of the Court. Also, the opinions in the cases hardly bear upon the subject of banking legislation. The question of the application of the Constitution goes beyond the mere validity of the laws which have been, or may be, enacted, and has a direct bearing upon the solution of the problem as to the proper method of creating and regulating the institutions through which the monetary process in this nation must be conducted. A system of government which has evolved from nearly a century and a half of control by the Constitution has had great effect upon the business, as well as the political, habits of the people of the United States. Any monetary system established should be in harmony with our system of government, as well as with the business and political habits of the people. It is almost certain that such harmony has not existed since the monetary system of Alexander Hamilton was abandoned, that of Andrew Jackson having begun — with a slight departure from the principles within the contemplation of the members of the Constitutional Convention of 1787 — a gradual trend which has gone far away from the true principles which were written into the Constitution by such great statesmen as George Washington, Alexander Hamilton, John Marshall, Benjamin Franklin, and James Madison, among others. The Constitution has been erroneously interpreted — although perhaps it should be said at once that this is not intended as a criticism of the *decisions* in the Gold Clause Cases.

There were two aspects of the situation in March of 1933 which must be given full significance. The first is that the occasion of the legislation to be considered was an emergency, and the second is that the very nature of the existing laws on money and banking not only was partly responsible for the emergency, but to a greater extent responsible for the erroneous ideas which were followed in the preparation of the bills enacted by Congress.

There were prevalent two great fallacies, general acceptance of which, not only by the public but by those in positions of leadership, had a tendency to force the Government into taking many steps which otherwise would have been more calmly considered, and prevented. The first of these fallacies was that falling prices were a cause, rather than a result of other causes, of the depression; and the second was that business leadership, in both finance and industry, was another cause of the depression. Directly attributable to the first fallacy was the price-raising monetary policy of the Administration; and all its proposals for restrictive legislation, which prevented the making of contracts at a time when the general tendency should have been toward freedom of contract, were as directly related to the second fallacy. All the advisers of the Government seem to have been thoroughly imbued with both fallacies, and how little they understood the actual conditions confronting them is well illustrated by the following part of the absurd preamble to one of the restrictive laws they persuaded Congress to enact.[1]

National emergencies, which produce widespread unemployment and the dislocation of trade, transportation, and industry, and which burden interstate commerce and adversely affect the general welfare, are precipitated, intensified, and prolonged by manipulation and sudden and unreasonable fluctuations of security prices and by excessive speculation on such exchanges and markets, and to meet such emergencies the Federal Government is put to such great expense as to burden the national credit.

The fact that all the banks in the country were closed at the time a new President was inaugurated, although an unfortunate consequence of at least twelve years of Government with little intelligence and a severe handicap to a new Administration, was merely one of the symptoms of prevailing conditions. It is doubtful whether any system of private banks could have continued to perform contracts to pay money on demand under the circumstances. The general suspension of such payments was not attributable to unsound banks, but to the policies of the Government itself, as explained in the preceding chapter. There was much talk of "the breakdown

[1] Securities Exchange Act.

of the capitalistic system", and apparently a general failure to understand that it was the *contractual* system which was in difficulties, largely on account of the fact that one of its fundamental rules, freedom of contract, had been violated. From that misunderstanding it was a comparatively easy step, either through ignorance or design, to the abrogation of another important rule of the system — that contracts shall be inviolable.

A wonderful opportunity to initiate a correct and permanent reform of the banking laws of the United States was missed. The Government should have proceeded to act according to the direct and plenary powers it had over the business of banking. Also it is obvious that the National Government should not ever attempt to exercise with the states concurrent control over any activity, and this is especially true of an emergency. There was one part of the banking business over which the National Government had the power to assume exclusive control. Over another part it had not the power to assume control exclusively. From the latter field it should have withdrawn, and at the same time it should have driven the states from the field over which the national jurisdiction should be supreme and exclusive. The discussion involves a survey of the two fields, and location of the dividing line between them. Preliminary to that, it may not be amiss to give here a summary of some aspects of national banking legislation which were considered in Chapter V.

National banks had been established, to furnish a national circulation of promises to pay coined money, and to do the commercial banking business of the country. At first it was thought that their privilege of issuing notes secured by United States bonds would enable them to drive state banks from competition in commercial banking, which was then regarded as being almost entirely dependent upon the note-issuing privilege. The original intention that they should acquire a monopoly of that part of the banking business was not accomplished, however; although it was expressed again by the Act of 1866, which taxed state bank notes out of existence. Failure to accomplish the purpose then, as well as much of the ever-present confusion about both money and banking, must not be ascribed to a want of constitutional power in Congress, but to a lack of understanding of the real nature of commercial banking.

It is important to note also that there had not

ever been any intention for the National Government to assume exclusive control of that part of the banking business which consists of the making of contracts by banks to pay money at a date certain, ordinarily called "the receipt of time deposits", or "savings accounts." With respect to that, the National Government had not attempted to do more than to authorize the financial institutions which it created to engage in making such contracts. There was a field from which state banks could not be driven.

The Constitution does not directly grant to the Congress any power either to establish or to regulate banks. Also, there is no general grant of power to Congress to enact laws relating to the making of any kind of contracts. That the power to establish a bank existed by necessary implication was, however, clearly demonstrated by both Alexander Hamilton and John Marshall. The unanimous opinion of the Supreme Court, in the case upholding the constitutionality of the Act of 1886 which destroyed state bank notes, shows that the power to regulate may be applied to banks other than those established under national laws, provided they make contracts to pay on demand. Alexander Hamilton announced the principle that the power to tax included the power to create money, and from that deduced that Congress had power to establish a bank. In his opinion sustaining the constitutionality of the Act of Congress which established the second Bank of the United States, Chief Justice Marshall followed the same line of reasoning, saying that if the bank was considered necessary by Congress for the *"fiscal operations"* of the National Government, creation of the bank was a proper exercise of power given by the Constitution.[2] The privilege of engaging in the business of making contracts to pay money is, under the system of the common law, one open to every citizen, or group of citizens, and anyone may establish a bank unless restrained by statute.[3] Engaging in the business of making contracts to pay money at a fixed time, as savings banks do, does not interfere in any effective manner with the "fiscal operations" of the National Government. Therefore, Congress has no power to enact a statute which excludes from that part of the field of banking anyone, except an institution created by national law, and must leave to the states enactment of such

[2] M'Culloch *v.* Maryland, 4 Wheaton 316.
[3] Noble State Bank *v.* Haskell, 219 U. S. 104, at 113.

statutes. Any institution which engages in the business of making contracts to pay money on demand does affect the "fiscal operations" of the National Government, and may interfere with, hinder, delay, and obstruct such operations, as has frequently been the case with banks. It seems advisable to consider further the ways in which that interference may occur and has occurred.

The ability of a government to create money is measured by its taxing power; but at the same time that it provides a means for the payment of its own dues it furnishes a means for the transaction of all business, and the supply must be adequate for both purposes. Institutions which engage in the business of making contracts to pay money on demand may either facilitate the entire monetary process, so that a comparatively small amount of money will answer all purposes, or they may restrain the process, so that the Government must create more money to serve both its own needs and those of business. When contracts of the banks to pay money on demand are unquestionably good, the public entrusts money to them, retaining in its own hands no more than is necessary for immediate needs; but when those contracts become doubtful, the public retains money for more remote needs, and hoarding begins. The wave of bank failures in the first part of 1933 was easily predicted by the steady rise in the amount of money in circulation, which became more perceptible in the latter part of 1932. Moreover, any institution the business of which consists of making contracts to pay money on demand must retain as a reserve with which to meet its promises an amount of money which bears some reasonable proportion to the amount which it may be called upon to pay. Certainly it may not be doubted that the National Government has the power to say where and how that reserve shall be kept, and, when it establishes a place for the keeping of such reserves, may declare who shall be permitted to patronize it. If only good banks engage in this particular branch of business, then the National Government is not called upon to place an undue strain upon its power to create money; but if unsound banks engage in it, the Government always becomes subjected to strong, almost undeniable, pressure to create more money, even at the risk of going beyond the breaking point for its own credit. The whole situation on March 4, 1933, both as to the banks and as to the currency, afforded the most perfect illustration of the principles here stated which could be found in all history. Consequently, it may be said that the grant to Congress of the power "to lay and collect Taxes" gives all needful authority, not only to create money, but to control the business of making contracts to pay money on demand. It seems better to ascribe the existence of both powers to that clause of the Constitution, as they are then both clear and plenary. Although both Hamilton and Marshall, in considering the constitutionality of bank legislation, placed some reliance upon the power of Congress "to regulate Commerce with foreign Nations, and among the several States", they were not considering the question of exclusive control of any part of the banking business. More recent discussion of the latter question has hardly been clarified by references to either the commerce clause or to the one which grants to Congress the power "to coin Money, regulate the Value thereof." . . . Both, however, could be used to support the argument here made.

If, during the "banking holiday", the Government had proceeded according to the principles above stated, it would have permitted national banks only to reopen for the transaction of commercial business. Undoubtedly it would have been necessary to announce the intention of removing both national banks and the National Government from the field of operations for savings banks, and of returning that to the states. The reopening of state banks as savings banks was a matter for the states. Either the Federal Reserve Banks, or the Reconstruction Finance Corporation, could have been made agents to conduct the demand deposit business of the state banks while they decided whether to obtain charters and resume business as national banks, or to become savings banks only. Such business could have been conducted with the regular employees of the state banks as employees of the agent for that particular purpose, and in the same premises formerly used. Making the demand deposits of closed institutions available to some extent for the transaction of new business could have been worked out by the agent in charge.

The making of contracts to pay money on demand was assignable to national banks as their exclusive and sole function. All other parts of the banking business properly come within the jurisdiction of the states. The separation of these functions would have required time, and many readjustments among the banks. In the meantime, communities without banks could have been provided for by giving either the Comptroller of the Currency or the Federal Reserve Board power to require any national bank to establish a branch wherever required by public convenience and necessity.

Such a banking system would have been workable, although with many of its features temporary. A general trend in the right direction was within the contemplation of this method of dealing with the situation, and such a course was far away from that of subsequent legislation, such as the guarantee of bank deposits.

There was in March 1933 almost as great a lack of confidence in the currency of the country as there was with reference to its banks. While distrust of the latter kind had caused hoarding of money, the fear of the unsoundness of the whole monetary system had caused hoarding of gold. As has been previously observed, all the legal arrangements relating to gold were cumbersome and obsolete. The action of the President in calling in the gold must be regarded as both wise and prompt. It is not necessary to distinguish between the executive orders and the Act of Congress which conferred the authority to proceed with them. The power in Congress to compel all gold to be turned in to the Treasury may easily be derived either from the commerce clause, with the view that the most important use of the gold was in commerce with other nations, or from the clause providing for the coinage of money, on the theory that in the opinion of Congress its use for the purpose of creating money was necessary.

The Act of 1933 which was passed to deal with the banking emergency went beyond requiring all owners of gold to sell it to the Treasury for any kind of "lawful money" tendered. It relieved the Treasury of its duty to sell gold, and made the export of gold for purposes of foreign trade subject to the discretionary granting of licenses. There was the first mistake. When the executive orders relating to gold had been complied with, the Treasury had more than four thousand million dollars' worth of the precious metal, which was the greatest hoard of gold ever known in the history of the world. To what use could it be put? The practical answers to that question reveal the whole situation in its true light.

It was soon demonstrated that the power of the United States to create money was ample for all purposes, even if it had not one single ounce of gold. The internal circulation of money in the United States required not a dollar's worth of gold for its support, and no set of circumstances could have shown that more forcibly than what happened during March and the first part of April. There was no loss of purchasing power by the dollar, although no one could buy any gold with it for internal use, and a purchase for external use was subject to license. The country sent abroad so many more goods than it received that the shipment of gold to balance payments with other nations was unnecessary. Therefore, the Government had no legitimate excuse for refusing to sell the gold.

The only reasonable uses to which the gold could be put were in the arts, industry, and for buying goods from other nations. Arrangements were made for the first two, but that would absorb a small quantity only; and the solution to the whole problem lay in selling the gold to other nations. The nature of the attempts to find remedies was controlled by the price-raising fallacy, which seems to have influenced the Government so much largely on account of the fact that spokesmen for the farmers believed in the fallacy so thoroughly. In shouting for devaluation of the dollar, the farmers were ill-advised. Their deplorable condition called for a remedy, and deserves some further consideration.

As has been argued in the preceding chapter, the plight of the farmers was largely attributable to the fact that they were denied freedom of contract in exchanging their products in the markets of the world for the goods which they needed. The law of the land was in effect that they could not sell abroad unless they brought back gold. All the gold had been drained out of the markets in which the farmers had previously been accustomed to sell. Obviously, it was a much better remedy for them to restore their markets by placing in those markets some of the unusable gold held by the Government of the United States than it was to raise the price of gold or devaluate the dollar. The effect of the one would be to restore the market for their surplus, which they were by natural justice entitled to produce, and the effect of the other would be merely to raise the price of the small amount which they could sell abroad under the conditions prevailing.

Raising the price of gold might give the farmers a temporary advantage, but it could not enable them to keep up with a procession of rising prices. The last thing they wanted was inflation on a "gold base", which according to the usual habit in the United States of creating several paper dollars out of each dollar's worth of gold might be expected to follow expansion of the gold base by devaluation. If four thousand millions of gold are changed by law to more than seven thousand millions, on the forty per cent. reserve principle there can be a terrific expansion of paper money. When that causes all other internal prices to rise, it cannot cause much of a rise in farm prices, as they are determined to a great extent by the gold price at which the exportable surplus is sold abroad. Under such circumstances, even if the farmer can sell abroad at a gold price that does not rise with the prices of things which he must buy, he is left behind. It is noticeable that the farm problem grew more acute all during the grand peacetime inflation under the Federal Reserve Act, and this seems to be an explanation of one cause of it. Should the farmers of the United States ever come to a real comprehension of the relations of money and the tariff to the prices which they obtain they would become the most ardent advocates of "hard money" and "free trade" this country has ever known.

There was just one way to place some of the surplus gold held by the United States in the markets where it could be used to buy the products of the farms of this country. That was by lowering the tariff. Thus the choice was between decreasing the demand for gold, — that is, lowering the ratio of exchange between it and other commodities in commerce among nations, which could be done by breaking the corner on the market built up by the United States and dumping its gold on the market, — and, on the other hand, yielding to the temptation to raise the price of gold by devaluating the dollar.

The choice of the latter course was an unfortunate result of the failure to comprehend the monetary process as involving something more than the bartering of gold for goods. With the Government of the United States levying and collecting more than three thousand million dollars a year in taxes, and other branches of government almost double that amount, it should have been obvious to any statesman that the "thing", whatever it was, used as a means of paying those taxes, had a great amount of purchasing power which was not in any way dependent upon gold. Furthermore, it was perfectly apparent that the dollar, if it was nothing more than a means of paying national, state, and local taxes in this country, had an ability to buy gold far in excess of the price which would be set by any law depreciating the dollar and raising the price of gold. Then there was also the internal debt paying power of the dollar, whether it was in a form which was legal tender in private payments or not, which was another overlooked distinction between the circulation of gold and that of the dollar. If it had been impossible to pay either taxes or debts in the United States with anything other than dollars made of 23.22 grains of pure gold, then there might have been some excuse for placing an embargo upon shipments of gold; but such was not the case. There was a plentiful supply of money created upon the credit of the Government. The policy which was begun with the Banking Act of 1933 was the result of the usual error in monetary legislation in the United States, a failure to distinguish between the internal circulation of money and the external circulation of gold.

Instead of a law which would have placed commercial banking where it belonged, under exclusive national control, there was created the Federal Deposit Insurance Corporation to guarantee all banks' contracts to pay money. Regardless of whether or not Congress has power to create such a corporation for the purpose of guaranteeing contracts of state banks to pay money at a fixed time, although a logical interpretation of the Constitution seems to justify a denial of such power, it was a mistaken policy to complicate the national system by bringing in savings banks, which are purely local institutions. The Act permitted further unnecessary complications of the same kind by providing that savings banks and small installment loan banks might become members of the Federal Reserve System. Such provisions showed a deplorable lack of comprehension of the nature of the monetary process and of the functions of the instruments through which it is to be conducted.

At a time when the policy of restricting freedom of contract had done incalculable harm, instead of reversing the tendency this Act imposed an additional restriction, in requiring that all contracts to ship gold abroad should be under license. The Act should have created a uniform national currency consisting of one kind of note and subsidiary coins. Then the gold should have been placed in the Federal Reserve System and made free for sale to all comers at the old price. An abandonment of the gold-reserve principle and adoption of that of the Fiduciary Issue would have shown everyone that there was no need to raise the price of gold.

After a start in dealing with an emergency according to incorrect principles, further retrogression came instead of progress. As if the restrictions upon the making of contracts in commerce among nations had not caused enough unemployment, the Government of the United States set about imposing some restrictions upon freedom of contract in its own internal commerce and industry. The Securities Act, the Agricultural Adjustment Act, and the National Industrial Recovery Act were all restrictions upon the making of contracts by which alone unemployment could be relieved. Those Acts are not to be considered as within the present subject, however, except to note that they were largely the result of the two fallacious ideas mentioned in the beginning of this chapter. No one in Washington seemed to comprehend the fact that men who had capital had to be permitted to make contracts in order that the unemployed might be put to work performing those contracts. All the laws which might be written to enforce collective bargaining for labor and higher prices for farmers were worthless if the market places for both were to be destroyed. The Recovery Act made revision of the tariff almost impossible, and was a very poor substitute for it.

The next result of the price-raising fallacy was the notorious Resolution of Congress on June 5, 1933, declaring all promises to pay in gold coin void. Part of it was well within the power of Congress, and part beyond the Constitution. As the Resolution was prepared on an erroneous theory as to the nature of the power of Congress over money, which should have been noticed and condemned by the Supreme Court but was not mentioned, it seems necessary to quote and analyze the Resolution. Its main body was as follows: —

Every provision contained in or made with respect to any obligation which purports to give the obligee a right to require payment in gold or a particular kind of coin or currency, or in an amount in money of the United States measured thereby, is declared to be against public policy; and no such provision shall be contained in or made with respect to any obligation hereafter incurred. Every obligation, heretofore or hereafter incurred, whether or not any such provision is contained therein or made with respect thereto, shall be discharged upon payment, dollar for dollar, in any coin or currency which at the time of payment is legal tender for public and private debts.

Any such provision contained in any law authorizing obligations to be issued by or under authority of the United States, is hereby repealed, but the repeal of any such provision shall not invalidate any other provision or authority contained in such law.[4]

This law must be considered as it affects the bonded indebtedness of the United States, first; and then as it affects private obligations. As to the former, all that need be said is that the power to declare how Government payments shall be made was in Congress and was exercised. To the extent that there was repudiation there is no legal remedy except as one has been, or may be, granted by Congress. No action either to enforce a contract or to recover damages for its breach may be brought against a sovereign government without its consent. So far as the law which permits the Court of Claims to hear cases against the United States gives the permission of Congress to render judgment on bonds payable in gold dollars of 23.22 grains pure, it might have been considered as amended or repealed to that extent by this Resolution. The Act was done irrevocably, and most members of Congress who voted for it will probably live to regret that they ever be-

[4] 48 Statutes at Large 113; U. S. Code Anno., Title 31, Sec. 463.

lieved it was either necessary or expedient. A decision which ended this phase of the matter should have been rendered, as is suggested in the separate opinion of Justice Stone in Perry *vs*. The United States.

As to private contracts to pay in "United States gold dollars of the present standard of weight and fineness" made when the standard was 23.22 grains per dollar, it may well be asked whether such promises have not always been void. Certainly they have been since the Act of 1901.[5] That Act declared it to be the policy of the United States to maintain all kinds of money issued by its authority "at a parity" with each other, and made it the duty of the Secretary of the Treasury to maintain that parity. Under such circumstances, if not under any circumstances when there is more than one kind of money, it required no Act of Congress to make contracts to pay in any particular kind of money void as against public policy. They had been so all along, as they were directly contradictory of an expressed national policy, since 1901 at least. Whenever a nation is foolish enough to place in circulation several different classes of paper currency, as was the case in the

[5] Quoted in full in Chapter V. See Note 16.

United States, the prevalence of the habit of making contracts to pay in a particular form of currency may prevent the circulation of some kinds of money, and, on general principles of law, any such contract must necessarily be void, as against public policy.

The view expressed in the preceding paragraph rests upon the assumption that such contracts were in the nature of promises to pay money, which they were held to be by the Supreme Court. If they had been construed as contracts to deliver gold bullion, a commodity, in a form stamped with the Mint's certificate of weight and fineness, then the only remedy for a failure so to deliver was a judgment for damages. No court in the United States is accustomed to render decrees requiring specific delivery of a commodity when the subject matter of the litigation is breach of a contract to do so. It is to be remembered that common law actions for damages must, in this country, be tried in a court in which a jury assesses the damages, and the Supreme Court held that no damages could be proved. Also, impossibility of performance was made a good defense by the seizure of all gold.

It requires one more step to show the utter lack of necessity for the Resolution, so far as private contracts were concerned. Suppose the cases had arisen without the Resolution ever having been passed. Although there would have been some uncertainty in the situation, if the Gold Clause Bonds had been held to be contracts to deliver gold as a commodity there would have been no serious danger, as explained above. That is, the obligors in such contracts could not have been mulcted under the circumstances, as they had perfectly good defenses against claims for damages. On the other hand, consider how the cases would have stood, without the Resolution, if the promises were in the nature of contracts to pay money. So far as they called for payment in a particular kind of money they were void as being contrary to public policy, either *ab initio* or since 1901. Also, in this aspect, impossibility of performance was a defense. The promise to pay in gold coin being void, the question arises as to what kind of money could have been offered in discharge of such contracts. Although the Resolution purported to make a change in the law of legal tender, by declaring that "all . . . currencies of the United States (including Federal Reserve notes and circulating notes of . . . national banking associations) . . . shall be legal tender for all debts, public and private", that was beyond the power of Congress, as has been explained in Chapter V.

It is to be noticed that the recent Gold Clause Cases presented a situation entirely different from that presented by the first Legal Tender Cases. At the time greenbacks were first held to be legal tender, a dollar in that kind of paper money would not buy either 23.22 grains of gold or 371.25 grains of silver. When the Gold Clause Cases arose, however, a paper dollar would buy at least twice that much silver. Also, in 1884, when the last of the Legal Tender Cases was decided, a greenback dollar would buy 371.25 grains of pure silver. There was the time when the futility of gold clauses should have been pointed out by the Supreme Court, as no more was needed than to decide the case according to the plain language of the Constitution. It is to be regretted also that the Court did not adhere to the Constitution in its opinion in the Gold Clause Cases, and show that the Resolution of Congress was as void, futile, and useless as the gold clauses, so far as it relates to private contracts. The Legal Tender Cases should have been expressly overruled. As the gold clause bonds were always dischargeable by tender of coined silver dollars, the whole controversy was about nothing, and never would have arisen if the Constitution had been observed.

The most unfortunate result of the price-raising fallacy was that the erroneous conception of a "commodity dollar" was allowed to arrest a tendency of the nations to abandon tariff and currency depreciation wars. Instead of participating in an international conference for that purpose, the United States should have used its power to lead the way by giving to the world a monetary unit which could have been used freely as the basis of commerce among nations. Not to assume the duties of leadership was bad enough, and the action of the United States in refusing to sell gold for foreign commerce, just before the World Economic Conference was to meet, would have been a crime against the law of nations if there had been any such law. Restraining commerce by building up a corner on any necessary commodity has been a crime at common law for a long time, and since the Sherman Antitrust Law was enacted by Congress in 1890 it has been a criminal offense so to restrain commerce among the states in this country. Raising the price of gold and draining it from weaker nations, when they needed it and could use it, and we neither needed it nor could use it, was exactly the same kind of moral offense.

There might have been some reason in the theory of a "commodity dollar" and devaluation, if the system of Andrew Jackson had still been in use in this country — that is, if there had been no paper money superstructure on gold. The ability of the paper to serve most of the uses of gold internally was a clear warning that the gold-buying policy would do more harm than good. Adoption of that policy would not have occurred if there had been an understanding of the fact that in modern times the ability of a nation to create money depends, not upon its possession of or ability to obtain gold, but upon the amount of taxes it may normally collect.

This reversion to barter was carried into the Gold Reserve Act of 1934. Up to that time the President had not formally exercised the authority to devaluate the dollar by as much as fifty per cent. which had been conferred upon him by Congress in the first part of 1933. It was still not too late to reverse the trend by breaking the corner on gold and decreasing the demand for it. The Act provided, however, that the dollar should be devalued by raising the price of gold from $20.67 per ounce to as much as $35 and not more than double the old price.

The greatest defect of that Act is that it not only continues the Government as a dealer in gold, but makes it an exclusive one. In this respect it is not modern and "stream-lined", but mediæval and obsolete. Enough has been said on this subject in connection with the duties of a Central Bank.

Another danger in the Act is that it will provide the means of repeating the same old story in the United States — coming out of a depression with arrangements for more inflation than that which collapsed to make conditions so severe, and thus insuring that the next depression will be worse than the preceding one. Moreover, the Act still clings to the obsolete and dangerous gold-reserve principle in permitting the Secretary of the Treasury to issue gold certificates which may be used by the Federal Reserve Banks as collateral for issuing two-and-one-half times their amount in money. It must be remembered that Congress has now declared Federal Reserve notes to be legal tender for all purposes. The danger of this gold reserve principle when at work on a "gold base" of eight thousand millions is appalling.

So far as real reform of the monetary system of

the United States is concerned, the Gold Reserve Act deals with some symptoms, on mistaken principles, instead of giving attention to primary causes. Its abolition of gold coins is probably a wise provision, but making the use of gold in commerce among nations dependent upon the discretion of a political officer of the Government is disturbing and unwise.[6]

[6] Except to the extent permitted in regulations which may be issued hereunder by the Secretary of the Treasury with the approval of the President, no currency of the United States shall be redeemed in gold: *Provided, however,* That gold certificates owned by the Federal Reserve banks shall be redeemed at such times and in such amounts as, in the judgment of the Secretary of the Treasury, are necessary to maintain the equal purchasing power of every kind of currency of the United States.

— 48 Statutes at Large, 340. U.S.C.A., Title 31, Sec. 408-a.

The Secretary of the Treasury shall, by regulation issued hereunder, with the approval of the President, prescribe the conditions under which gold may be acquired and held, transported, melted or treated, imported, exported, or earmarked: (*a*) for industrial, professional, and artistic use; (*b*) by the Federal Reserve banks for the purpose of settling international balances; and, (*c*) for such other purposes as in his judgment are not inconsistent with the purposes of section 441 and this section. Gold in any form may be acquired, transported, melted or treated, imported, exported, or earmarked or held in custody for foreign or domestic account (except on behalf of the United States) only to the extent permitted by, and subject to the conditions prescribed in, or pursuant to, such regulations. Such regulations may exempt from the provisions of this section, in whole or in part, gold situated in the Philippine Islands or other places beyond the limits of the continental United States.

— 48 Statutes at Large, 340. U.S.C.A., Title 31, Sec. 442.

Are these statutes constitutional? They seem to be, for the following reasons: to regulate commerce with foreign nations

As if the effect of the policies of the United States with respect to gold had not created disturbance enough in the countries which had been accustomed to try to operate on a gold standard, the Government made an impartial distribution of the effects of its destructive policies, by turning its attention to silver. By the Act of June 19, 1934, it was declared that "the proportion of silver to gold in the monetary stocks of the United States should be increased, with the ultimate object of having and maintaining one fourth of the monetary value of such stocks in silver." The "monetary value" of silver is at present theoretically fixed at one dollar and twenty-nine and

Congress may establish an agency to buy and sell gold for the facilitation of that commerce; the fact that the arrangement made impedes instead of facilitating reveals only the folly of choosing the particular method, and not a lack of power so to act. It being definitely established that Congress has power to establish an agency to deal in the precious metals, and, as pointed out by Hamilton in his memorandum to Washington on the constitutionality of the Act incorporating the first Bank of the United States, such an agent may be either a bank or the National Treasury, it follows that the power cannot be qualified with a requirement that either sales or purchases be made at a fixed price. Obviously Congress cannot decide upon changes in the prices, if changes are to be made, and there seems to be no reason for denying the authority to delegate to the Secretary of the Treasury the power to fix and alter the prices. Perhaps delegating authority to fix the metallic content of coins presents a different question.

nine-tenths cents per ounce, which is according to the number of grains coined into a silver dollar. That means that the United States must hoard approximately two thousand million ounces of silver, as the Secretary of the Treasury is authorized and *directed* "to purchase silver at home or abroad" to accomplish the purpose of the Act. He is not authorized to sell it until "the market price of silver exceeds its monetary value", the former now being less than one half of the latter, or until the "monetary value" of the silver hoarded exceeds one fourth of the monetary value of the hoards of both gold and silver. Naturally the efforts of the Treasury to carry this Act into effect have raised the price of silver, not only in this country but in all others. The far-reaching results of this policy, extending to all countries on a silver standard, may be illustrated by the conditions in China.

The currency of China has consisted largely of silver coins, the Government of that country not being strong enough to supply any kind of currency other than a metallic one. A high price for silver offered in the United States tends to cause silver to be exported from China, and thus the country is deprived of the only money it can have. An export tax of fifteen per cent. was imposed upon the export of silver from China, but that has not been sufficient to prevent the drain. "Two banks recently failed in Shanghai within a week, one of them a five hundred thousand dollar institution, and within the space of a month there has been a drop of twenty-five per cent. in the weaving and spinning trades, thirty per cent. in hat making, forty per cent. in dye-stuffs, fifty per cent. in ironwork and glass ware, and thirty-five per cent. in rubber goods." [7] All this, of course, cannot be charged against the silver buying of the United States, but it does show convincingly the error in the argument of the advocates of the "remonetization" of silver that an increase in the price of silver would increase the "purchasing power" of the people in countries on a silver standard. Furthermore, it gives sad proof of the extent to which the Government of the United States lacks both the intelligence and the sense of responsibility necessary for international leadership.

In countries on a silver standard, the results of recent legislation of the United States affecting silver have been comparable to those of the unfor-

[7] Editorial in the *New York Herald Tribune,* December 22, 1934.

tunate Act of 1834 in driving out of circulation all the minor coins of this country. It seems that the members of Congress might have been familiar enough with the financial history of their own country not to make such a mistake again. Making the mistake so it affects other countries is one thing, however, and making it so that it causes all dimes, quarters, and half-dollars in this country to be withdrawn from circulation because their bullion value exceeds their legal value is another. The silver half-dollar contains 192.9 grains of standard silver, and quarters and dimes one-half and one-fifth of that amount.[8] When, and if, the price of silver goes to the point for which the aim of the Treasury seems set, $1.299 per standard ounce, the half-dollar coin will contain silver worth fifty-two and eight one-hundredths cents, which will offer sufficient profit to cause all silver subsidiary coins to be melted for sale as bullion, in defiance of any law. The Silver

[8] The silver coins of the United States shall be a dollar; a half-dollar, or fifty-cent piece; a quarter-dollar, or twenty-five-cent piece; and a dime, or ten-cent piece. The weight of the dollar shall be four hundred and twelve and one-half grains troy of standard silver, the weight of the half-dollar shall be one hundred and ninety-two and nine-tenths grains; the quarter-dollar and the dimes shall be, respectively, one-half and one-fifth of the weight of said half-dollar.

— R.S. 3513: U.S.C.A., Title 31, Sec. 316.

Purchase Act contains a provision authorizing the President to decrease the silver content of these coins, but to call them all in for a recoinage will illustrate the height of folly, and may subject the people to great inconvenience.

The great mistake is that the power of this nation is being misused to increase the price of both metals, when it should be used to decrease the price of gold. Where the true interests of the silver people really point is toward a readjustment of the open-market ratio of exchange between the two metals. To some extent that conflicts with the interests of all other people, but there are possibilities of compromise, on sound principles, for the benefit of all. At present the United States is leading the way in exerting the power of all important nations to increase the price of gold, which of course makes the open-market ratio go against silver. The United States is alone, however, in exerting power to increase the price of silver; and thus, so far as the open-market ratio between the two metals is concerned, its efforts in one direction are offset by those in another. It is probable that the natural open-market ratio of exchange between gold and silver — that is, when no power of any government is being used to affect the price of either metal — is not more than from twelve to sixteen to one in favor of gold; whereas at present the ratio is around forty-nine to one, the price of gold being thirty-five dollars per ounce and of silver about seventy-three cents. If the United States should reverse its policy with reference to gold, throwing it on the market instead of hoarding it, which is what should be done, then the open-market ratio to silver would fall greatly. The silver "bloc" in Congress would have been consistent, and wiser, if it had voted against increasing the price of gold. Should the United States, however, adopt free coinage of silver at the rate of sixteen to one, and thereby establish a silver standard, the consequence would be money steadily increasing in open-market value, and constantly falling prices so far as monetary effects on prices are concerned. First, there would be a shift to a silver standard; and the power of the United States would gradually be used to increase the price of silver in terms of other commodities. A silver standard would thus become as unpopular as any gold standard has been. In fact, if the United States should adopt free coinage of both metals at the ratio of sixteen to one, it is not at all improbable that within a few years there would occur an automatic shift back to a gold standard. The fact that silver legislation in the United States is to-day entirely different from what it was forty years ago, on account of the tremendous increase in the ability of the Government to affect the price of precious metals, must be taken into consideration. So far as the metals are concerned, the proper course for the United States to pursue would be to depress the price of gold and remain neutral as to silver, except to use it for such coins as are necessary for internal circulation.

All recent monetary legislation in the United States has simply tended to prevent the dollar from serving as a means of establishing a Standard of International Trade. In the first part of 1933, the dollar did not offer any hope of providing a good Standard, but there was not any other immediate prospect. Legislation wisely prepared could easily have made it a monetary unit which would buy gold at its century-old price, and one which could be bought with the goods of other nations. That would have revived the making of contracts in commerce among nations; and agriculture, commerce, and industry in the United States would have given better relief to the unemployed of this country than the

Government has been able to give. Destruction of the Standard for commerce among nations, and serious impairment of the internal standard, have done the people of this country an incalculable amount of harm. It is impossible to believe that the level of their intelligence is so low as to be fairly represented by the monetary system now in existence and the policies of the Government with respect to commerce among nations during the last fourteen years.

With the Banking Act of 1935, the long trek backward in monetary legislation has carried us from the excellent system attributable largely to the wisdom of George Washington and Alexander Hamilton to one very similar to that established by Great Britain in 1816. That country then tried, from 1816 to 1844, both the gold-reserve principle and Central Bank management of currency. Bitter experience demonstrated that those principles would not work successfully, although in other respects the British system of that period seems to have been superior to our present one. The great defects of the Banking Act of 1935 are that it continues the Government as a dealer in gold; that is retains the gold-reserve principle of the Federal Reserve Act, without limit except in the forty per cent. gold requirement; and that it is founded upon an unreasonable belief in the efficacy of an attempt at centralized control of the desires and fears of men to make contracts to pay money. To accomplish such control, the authors of the Act relied upon delegation to the Federal Reserve Board of the powers to direct the open-market operations of the Reserve Banks and to change the reserve requirements for member banks.[9]

As the Gold Reserve Act of 1934 is an effective

[9] The Act creates a Federal Open Market Committee which consists of the members of the Board of Governors of the Federal Reserve System and five representatives of the Federal Reserve Banks. It then provides: —

No Federal Reserve bank shall engage or decline to engage in open-market operations under section 14 of this Act except in accordance with the direction of and regulations adopted by the Committee. The Committee shall consider, adopt, and transmit to the several Federal Reserve banks, regulations relating to the open-market transactions of such banks. The time, character, and volume of all purchases and sales of paper described in section 14 of this Act as eligible for open-market operations shall be governed with a view to accommodating commerce and business and with regard to their bearing upon the general credit situation of the country.

With respect to control of reserve requirements for Member Banks, the Act provides: —

Notwithstanding the other provisions of this section, the Board of Governors of the Federal Reserve System, upon the affirmative vote of not less than four of its members, in order to prevent injurious credit expansion or contraction, may by regulation change the requirements as to reserves to be maintained against demand or time deposits or both by member banks in reserve and central reserve cities or by

prevention of the existence of a Standard of International Trade, and the Banking Act of 1935 makes no improvement in that respect, any extensive consideration of the latter seems unnecessary. The two Acts continue in effect an organization of monetary and banking institutions which, at the time of their enactment, had been proved to be defective through experience; and both Acts tend to make probable another inflation on a gold base. In this connection, it is remarkable that when the opponents of the Banking Act of 1935 were charged by its advocates with being the same old group of conservatives who had opposed the Federal Reserve Act in 1913, and with their having been mistaken then as proof that they were wrong again, there was no reply that they were right in 1913. The next expansion of contracts to pay money on a margin of forty per cent. in gold, and the inevitable deflation afterwards, may teach the people of the United States not to enact laws which permit and encourage the process of inflation.

---

member banks not in reserve or central reserve cities or by all member banks; but the amount of the reserves required to be maintained by any such member bank as a result of any such change shall not be less than the amount of the reserves required by law to be maintained by such bank on the date of enactment of the Banking Act of 1935 nor more than twice such amount.

CHAPTER VIII

A DISCUSSION OF PRINCIPLES

In trying to ascertain, theoretically, the correct principles to be adopted in the preparation of laws providing for the creation of money, it is necessary to keep in mind these facts: the monetary process is carried on through three instruments, contracts, money, and banks; and of these the most important is the contract. The other two are merely facilitating instruments, money an artificial one, and a bank one which inevitably develops out of a contractual system operating according to the natural laws of barter. In the making and performance of contracts, there may be just as much facilitation from the use of a customary and standard commodity medium of exchange as from the use of money. No law is needed to make that commodity standard, but only a general desire of men to possess it. Also banks may just as readily, conveniently, and profitably, to society as well as to themselves, engage in the business of making contracts to deliver the standard commodity medium of exchange as in that of making contracts to pay money.

The development of banking does not involve a departure from the natural system of barter contracts. Bills of exchange and checks do not abolish barter, as they may be just as useful when orders to deliver the commodity medium of exchange as they are when orders to pay money, and fundamentally their nature does not differ in one case from the other. Furthermore, the exchange of a promise to deliver one commodity, used as a medium, for another commodity is still barter, and so is the exchange of a promise to deliver the one for a promise to deliver the other. It is a mistake, of great theoretical importance and sometimes of unfortunate practical consequences, to regard barter as being superseded when credit instruments are developed. In a contractual system operating on a barter basis with a standard commodity medium of exchange there are three classes of deliveries of that medium: from citizens to the government; from the government to citizens; and by citizens to each other. When money is created the classes of payments fall into the same division.[1]

[1] Knapp, "The State Theory of Money", p. 96.

The introduction of money into a contractual system operating according to the natural laws of barter causes the monetary process to operate on principles essentially different. Contracts and banks, being instruments more nearly natural so far as their creation is concerned, are not confined to national boundaries in their operations. Money, however, is strictly a national, internal instrument which can have no existence, as money, beyond its own national borders. This is not the only cause of distinctions set up by the creation of money.

It has been said that the certification by a government of the weight and fineness of a piece of a precious metal does not of itself create money, but when the government doing that will accept in payments due it all such pieces of metal, without use of the scales, money is created. The mere fact that a coin worn so as to have suffered an appreciable loss of weight will be accepted in payment of debts sets up a distinction between the internal and external circulations. If, however, this is the only fact existing to cause such a distinction, it amounts to little; and the circulation is still largely subject to the natural laws of barter. There is, under these circumstances, hardly more than an officially certified commodity medium of exchange. That commodity tends to be distributed both nationally and internationally, so far as a nation using such a system is concerned, on a barter basis.[2] If a government using as money nothing more than such an officially certified commodity medium of exchange confines it to one metal, and assumes the expense of keeping the coins up to full weight, — that is to say, receives lightweight coins but does not pay them out, — a system of this kind will work excellently — far better than most modern monetary systems. It is automatic in providing the particular country with the amount of money required for the conduct of its commerce and industry.

Great difficulties are experienced in the maintenance of such a system, however. It was a system of this kind that Andrew Jackson tried to establish in the United States. He made the mistake of not confining it to one metal, which under the circumstances, if there were to be any minor coins, should have been silver; but he tried to use gold also. The purity of the system later had to be abandoned by the creation of token subsidiary coins. Also Jackson's the-

---

[2] Ricardo so treats the subject in his "Political Economy", chapter on Foreign Trade.

ory of the Constitution prevented him from establishing a system purely of this kind, as he was forced to tolerate state bank notes, and many of the states accepted them in payment of taxes. In fact, some of the states went so far as to found banks for the express purpose of issuing notes receivable in payment of state taxes. Thus there were some possibilities of inflation in Jackson's system not to be expected in one of this kind, and to that extent it was not fully automatic.

The minute any kind of promises to deliver, or pay, this commodity medium of exchange is brought in and made receivable in tax payments, or legal tender in private payments, or both, as is usual, the automatic distribution of the medium with reference to other nations is prevented. In this connection payments should be considered as being for either of two general purposes: they are made either to acquire possession of things, including land, or to retain possession of them. The first kind of payment is involved directly in the vital question of prices, and must be considered as being broad enough to include the passing of money in both voluntary sales and the voluntary rendering of services. In transactions embraced within this class the parties on both sides act without legal compulsion, and the willing buyer and the willing seller, with bargaining between them, are still regarded as typical of all business transactions. That was the case before there occurred in nearly all modern nations the great expansion in the activities of governments, preceded, or accompanied by, increased complexity of social and industrial organization. All the facts involved in this trend of development have tended to decrease the comparative importance of payments of money made to acquire possession of things, and to increase comparatively the importance of payments made to retain possession. The greater part of the attention of students of monetary questions has been given to the first class, but the increasing frequency and total amount of payments of the latter class demand consideration.

Payments made to retain possession of things are mostly for taxes and debts. In general, it may be said that no matter how much depreciated a currency becomes it is good for these two purposes. That fact tends to give it some support in the retention of its ability to serve as a means of obtaining things, but in the case of a great depreciation that support is not enough to prevent great disparity between the debt-paying power of the money and its purchasing power. Of course, some of this effect may be prevented if the government issues such money to pay its own bills and refuses to accept it in payment of taxes. That does little more, however, than to increase the injustice of the whole procedure. The situation may be changed somewhat also if a depreciated currency is not made legal tender.

One point here which is overlooked by most inflationists is that a depreciated currency may be of advantage to those who have great possessions, whom it is not intended to help, as it serves them in retaining their wealth fully as well as a more valuable currency. On the other hand, it puts at a great disadvantage those who have little and must labor for money wages in order to get the goods they need, as the ability of an inflated currency to serve their purposes constantly decreases and they cannot hope to increase their supply of the currency according to their demands.

There is also a class of payments usually made to obtain temporary possession of things, or sometimes for personal services, which requires special attention. This class consists of those payments made to persons under obligation to give temporary use of facilities upon tender of a fixed price. Passenger and freight transportation on trains, and telephones and electric lights, are instances of things obtained by such payments. Here public regulation prevents free bargaining, and any depreciation of the currency damages all who are engaged in such businesses. They cannot raise the prices charged until permission of the public authorities is obtained. The tendency is to extend to a greater number of businesses the duty to serve all at charges subject to public regulation, and all engaged in such enterprises, whether as owners or employees, suffer from the liability of having legal tenders made in depreciated currency.

With respect to all these various classes of payments, the point is that they are potential sources of disturbing complications in the use of money whenever a government begins to create a kind of money different from the customary commodity medium of exchange. Without all the intricacies of government these complications do not exist, and that barter medium generally circulates in all classes of payments on the same principles. The mere existence of separate nations, however, sets up a distinction between the internal circulation of money and the circulation of the commodity medium of exchange which must still be used in the barter between any two nations. Commerce among the nations cannot be anything other than barter, as the money of one is in another a commodity only, or a mere claim subject to collection.

The creation by a government of enough money to cause a difference between its circulation, which ordinarily can be internal only, and that of the standard commodity medium of exchange, sets up complications in the making and performance of contracts long before any depreciation of that money begins. This is said on the assumption that the depreciation is measured by the ability of the money to buy the standard medium of exchange. As the creation of money different from that medium proceeds, although there is an apparently reasonable limitation upon the amount so created, there begins to arise, almost imperceptibly at first, a disparity between the ability of that money to obtain things and its ability to retain possession of them. Furthermore, its ability to obtain some things decreases, — that is, their prices rise, — while with respect to other things there is no such change. All this occurs more rapidly with such money than on account of the natural shifts in the distribution of a commodity medium of exchange. The complications set up by governments engaging in the creation of money seem to be that there is, first, a distinction caused between the internal and external circulation; then there come distinctions between the uses to which the money they create may be put in the various classes of payments, which of course are internal only.

Now a government has a vital interest in payments of money, since it is the receiver of the greatest amount paid to any one person or institution. In all nations of to-day tax payments exceed those to anyone other than the government. The government of any nation has no direct interest in exchanges of the standard commodity medium, or at least none which exceeds the interest it has in the exchange of other commodities. So long as it creates money prudently as a means of paying taxes, there is no necessity for a government to have any contact with the commodity used as a standard medium of exchange in commerce with other nations. The commonly accepted view of this feature of the process is, however, that the government must maintain the convertibility of all money it creates into the standard

commodity. That view is erroneous. What really occurs, when a government creates some money with
its credit and continues the use of a metallic medium
of exchange as money also, is that the standard metal
is bought and sold in prices payable with the other
class of money. The true purpose is to maintain the
ability of the money, which is created on the strength
of the taxing power, to buy the medium of exchange.
To accomplish that it is not necessary that the government buy or sell a single piece of the standard
metal, as the judgment of the open market is a far
better check on the soundness of the money than any
metallic reserve ever can be. At this point there
enters the question of a fixed price for the standard
metal. How can a government maintain that unless
it sells the metal?

Commerce among nations is not engaged in by
governments, but is a part of the business activities of its citizens. The Standard of International
Trade is not established in order that governments
may make or receive any kind of payment, and
if only a few of the more important ones begin to
try to use it for that purpose the Standard soon
disappears. A commodity medium of exchange continues to be used, after legally created money ap-

pears, for the purposes of commerce among nations only. As the money of one nation cannot be used to make a payment in another, it is necessary to send to the latter something which can be sold in order to obtain that nation's money. A fixed price for some standard thing generally sought after in all countries is desirable for facilitation in making and performing contracts in commerce among nations. Since those contracts are made in the course of the commercial activities of citizens, there are only two occasions for governmental interference with them: to make them a source of tax revenue, and to restrict them for one purpose or another. Taxes on such transactions can be collected in legally created money just as well as those on any other kind of business. Consequently, a government has no more excuse for dealing in one of the commodities involved in the making and performance of contracts in commerce among nations than it has for dealing in any of the commodities bought and sold in its internal commerce. The maintenance of a fixed price for the standard medium of exchange gives only an apparent reason for the government dealing in whatever happens to be that standard commodity. If possession of a metallic medium is not regarded as a means of creating money it is quickly seen that there is no reason for a government to buy and sell a metal. Dealing in gold, or any other metal, is purely a commercial activity, and should play no part in the creation of money.

On the other hand, the creation of money is a function of government exclusively. Just as governments should not participate in the commercial activities in which the standard commodity medium of exchange is used, so should all commercial, or business, institutions be excluded from the creation of money. Here it is necessary to distinguish clearly between the business of banking and the governmental function of creating money. The extent to which the two are confused is indicated by the prevalent use of the erroneous expression "deposit currency." Banks do not create money unless they are permitted to issue notes which are accepted by the government. Neither a contract to pay money nor an order to perform such a contract can be treated as money with the prospect of any correct reasoning following such an erroneous beginning. A check does not circulate as currency any more than it does as money, since it does not discharge a debt until the money is paid in partial performance of the contract of the existence of which it is a representation and against which it is drawn.

Consequently, so far as the creation of money is concerned, governments have two alternatives only, if correct principles are to be adopted. The first is to use nothing for the purpose except the standard commodity medium of exchange, in forms officially certified as to quantity and quality. To do that without any possibility of disturbing distinctions between the internal and external circulations, and among the various classes of internal payments, there should not even be a subsidiary token coinage. Bank notes should also be prohibited. These two difficulties make it almost impossible for any modern nation to use a system of this kind. Andrew Jackson attempted it for the United States, but tried to use gold coins for large denominations and silver for small coins, and allowed an erroneous construction of the Constitution to restrain the abolition of state bank notes.

The other method involves the use of government credit on correct principles. Here the confusion of commercial use of the standard commodity medium of exchange with the creation of money has given rise to the erroneous idea that the credit is properly used if the money is "backed" by a reserve of the metallic medium of exchange ranging from as low as twenty-five to as high as forty or fifty per cent. No matter how high the percentage of the reserve is, that portion of the money which exceeds the reserve rests upon nothing more than the credit of the government. In turn that credit rests upon nothing except the ability to collect taxes. Therefore, the purchasing power of any money created on government credit depends primarily upon the extent to which it must be used to retain possession of things as against the tax collector. From that it follows that the amount of money in existence should not exceed the normal and prudent annual operating expenses of government. Any amount of money created in excess of that is inflationary.

This second method requires that the price of the standard commodity medium of exchange be first allowed to find its own proper level with respect to prevailing conditions. Then the duty of buying and selling that commodity medium at a fixed price should be delegated to a Central Bank. That bank, however, should not be permitted to issue notes. Maintenance of the fixed price for the medium of exchange would, under such circumstances, be entirely dependent upon the existence and proper administration of a Standard for International Trade. Without aid from that source, no nation except the most powerful one can hope to continue this desirable feature of the system, a fixed price for the medium.

Naturally, the first step in beginning operations according to the second method is the establishment of a system of taxation. In doing that, the government announces that it will require certain payments to be made either on the occurrence of certain acts or annually from those who are in possession of land and things. Once it is made known that these levies and collections will be recurring, either annually or on each transaction in designated classes of business, the retention of possession of all land and things in the territory of the government depends upon being able to satisfy the levies by delivery of whatever thing is required by the government. The mere designation of that thing makes it money, and its physical attributes are best ignored in this immediate connection. Payment of expenses must begin before the collection of taxes, and if the government chooses it may so pay with a thing specially created for the collection of taxes, although probably at a loss. It is doubtful, however, whether the loss would exceed that involved in borrowing a sufficient quantity of the medium of exchange with which to begin such operations.

Suppose the government decides that in the beginning it will levy no taxes except those to be collected annually; that all taxes will come due one year from the date on which the law is announced; and it proceeds to create an issue of its own notes and token coins in an amount estimated to be that which it will collect at the end of the year. In order to ensure receiving them back, the notes and coins must be placed in circulation, and that will not be done in a satisfactory manner by retaining them in its treasury and paying out only as expenses are incurred. The attention of the government is then directed to those who have been engaged in the business of making contracts to deliver the commodity used as a medium of exchange, that is to say, the bankers. Probably there are many, some well established and of great prestige, and others weak. The officials of the treasury consider the problem of whether to deliver all the notes to one bank to be paid out as ordered, and let it lend them out for circulation, or to select a number of banks. Establishment of a government bank may seem a little venturesome under the circumstances, and it is decided that the best substitute for that is to select the strongest of the private banks.

An almost immediate result of depositing these notes in that bank is that contracts to deliver the medium of exchange are superseded by contracts to pay money. That may have been provided for by law, or left to work itself out from a new start. In the latter case the contracts to deliver the commodity medium of exchange would remain to be discharged, and that commodity would have to be bought with the money by those who had promised to deliver it. Also that commodity would practically cease to be used in internal exchanges, but its use in barter exchanges with other countries would continue. Furthermore, its price would be subject to fluctuations.

Under such circumstances it might be confidently expected that there would be a protest to the government against the fluctuating exchanges with other countries. That might be joined by the bankers, other than the ones selected by the government, with complaints against all the money being kept in one place, and their disadvantage with respect to competition with the favored bank. In all probability it would be suggested that the chosen bank should assume some responsibilities in consideration of the advantages given it. Such demands might well result in responsibilities being imposed upon the bank selected by the government to the following extent: —

1. That it assume the burden of selling at a fixed price the commodity formerly used as a medium in all exchanges, and now in those with other countries only; also that it agree to buy that commodity at the same price.

2. That it withdraw from competition with the other banks, make loans to them, and to no one else.

The second of these provisions could easily be incorporated into the law, and that would make a Central Bank of the one selected by the government. There would be some difficulty, however, in fixing a price for the commodity used as a medium of exchange with other nations. If it be assumed that the estimate of the government as to the amount of money to be created was approximately correct, the price would fall after the first disturbances of the innovation were over. Also, in a country of growing wealth and population, the price of this standard medium of exchange with other nations, probably gold, would tend to decline constantly if the amount of money remained unchanged. So would the price of all other commodities. In addition, the expenses of the government would increase. These facts would not only justify, but require, some future increase in money, and the manner in which that was to be provided for would have a direct bearing upon determination of the price of gold at the Central Bank.

It is to be emphasized that the amount of money originally created represented the government's normal and prudent annual operating expenses only. Interest and principal payments on past indebtedness, capital expenditures, and all extraordinary items were excluded. Also, that the expenses of subsequent years are to be paid by collecting the money in taxes, and not by creating more money. The amount of money should increase equally with the amount by which the government would be justified in increasing its normal annual operating expenses. (A distinction must be made between those expenses and the total expenditures of the government. For instance, although the total expenditures of the United States Government have been for some years above three thousand millions, its normal operating expenses are less than one thousand, five hundred millions.)

The problem would be to make the amount of money in existence always represent, approximately, that proportion of a country's production of real wealth which its government is justified in consuming as its normal operating expenses during one year. A reasonably accurate method of estimating the need for additional money would be to take an annual average for a few years from the following: at the end of any one year the additional sum of money to be created should bear the same proportion to that year's total savings in the nation as that borne by the normal operating expenses of the government to the total expenditures of the citizens for consumption. In a growing nation, that would provide for a healthy increase in money, and without increase in wealth there should be no additional money.

All that the foregoing is intended to be is a theoretical outline, as there are many additional problems, the treatment of which would require going into too many details for present purposes. The advantages and disadvantages of such a system, in comparison with those in use at present, also present a subject for discussion which must be neglected. Attention may be invited, however, to one probable result of following this theory of the creation of money. If it should be generally understood that money is created solely on the use of the taxing power, and that when correctly done it requires no hoard of metal, there might be an end to the controversy over whether the Government should buy one metal instead of another for monetary purposes. The fallacious idea that money may be created whenever "backed by" sufficient assets of the proper kind has done great damage. There will always be differences of opinion, both as to the sufficiency of such assets and as to whether one or another is of the proper kind.

Not much may be said about the theory which should be followed in the preparation of laws relating to banking without going into the practical aspects of the business, which is beyond the present subject. In one respect those laws present a question of great difficulty, but some comments may not be amiss. The very nature of the business of banking, which must always be regarded as that of making and performing contracts to pay money, places those who engage in it under the highest duty to the public when any great number of people begin to patronize banks. Yet the making of a contract to pay money is

essentially a private, personal affair. Most businesses
which are sometimes referred to as being "affected
with a public interest" are under an obligation to
serve all members of the public on the same terms.
The mere fact that they are engaged in a particular
business is sufficient to put some kinds of institutions
under the obligation of doing business. There never
has been a law requiring any bank, except when a
Central Bank is involved, to *make* any contract to pay
money, and from the very nature of the business
there cannot be such a law. It is not inconceivable
that a person might be unable to find any bank that
would receive his money and make a contract to pay
it on demand as ordered. There seems to be no law
requiring any bank to do so. All the laws are related
to forbidding the banks to make certain kinds of contracts, and to trying to ensure that they will perform
all their contracts legally made. The business appears to be a complicated mixture of private enterprise and public duty; but entering into contractual
relations is the private commercial part, and the performance of the contracts made is the public part.
There is an inherent difficulty in regulating any business in which the institutions involved cannot be
compelled to do business in any particular instance.

In addition, the terms upon which banks make contracts to pay money for others, in return for promises to repay it at a certain time, cannot be regulated successfully.

All the contracts of the banks are hardly more than ancillary to the making and performance of contracts to produce or to sell things, and to undertake projects. Contracts of the latter kind give the impetus to business activity, and the reasons for making them, as well as the existence or nonexistence of those reasons, are beyond the knowledge of any regulatory power of men. To attempt to promote the making of contracts to manufacture, to build, and to sell, by making it easy to make contracts to pay money, gives an undue emphasis to the instrument of lesser importance, to the neglect of the greater one. The individual motives in the making of all these contracts, including those to pay money made by the banks, keep the business of banking from being one which may be run according to rules set forth in statutes.

The disposition of the public to impose unwise regulatory laws upon banks comes largely from the impression that the banks create money. So they did, when permitted to issue notes receivable in payments to governments; but the only remaining vestige of that is when a Central Bank controlled by the private banks is permitted to issue such notes. When it is clearly understood that banks do no more than make contracts to pay money, the error of regarding them as creators of "deposit currency", and trying to force them to use it for the benefit of the public, will cease to cause such unfortunate results. It seems that it would help to remove many difficulties if all connections of Central Banks with the creation of money were severed. At the same time, governments should cease to deal in gold, and then the Central Banks should be left largely to the control of their private stockholder, or member, banks.

CHAPTER IX

REORGANIZATION

THE institutions through which the monetary process is conducted in the United States are all set for
another grand inflation whenever the restrictions
upon the making of contracts are either removed or
successfully evaded. It seems probable that within not
so many years one or the other of the conditions
necessary to start again the inflationary process will
arise. A belief that currency "management" can restrain the overexpansion of contracts to develop
natural resources in this country, from which the
overexpansion of contracts to pay money will result
unless there is a removal of inflationary possibilities
from the laws, is founded upon an underestimate of
the uses to which the real national wealth may be
put. Such a belief also overestimates the efficacy of
currency management, even if it is conscientiously
tried with intellectual honesty, which is most improbable with the power lodged in a politically constituted authority. There should be an immediate

and thorough reform of all national laws providing for the establishment and administration of monetary institutions.

The manner in which that reform should be attempted depends upon whether the United States will assume the duty of establishing and administering a Standard of International Trade. It seems hardly worth while, however, to discuss the question of revising the monetary laws unless there is to be a real Standard created. Without that, the situation is too uncertain and dangerous to justify a guess as to either what might happen or what should happen. The United States not only has the power to create and administer an International Standard, but it also has the power to prevent from working a Standard established by any other nation. Destructive use of the latter power has now been going on for several years, and the accusation that other nations fail to co-operate gives no excuse whatsoever. They cannot afford to take the risk of tying up to an unworkable Standard; and until there is one to which they may turn for support it is too difficult for them either to stabilize their currencies or to remove import restrictions. The United States can well afford to take the risk of leading the way, and of establishing a Standard to which the other nations would gladly attach themselves when given proof of a disposition on the part of the most powerful nation to assume the responsibility of making it a workable one. A question which the people of the United States should consider is, how long may a misused power be expected to last? Once the power to establish and administer a Standard is lost, the United States may expect not only to pay some other nation for administering a future Standard, but to become exposed to the dangers of being a secondary nation without friends and with enemies.

Another question of importance is, can the United States establish a Standard for commerce among nations? That it has the wealth, power, and stability of government necessary may hardly be denied. The two requisites which may be lacking are bankers of sufficient experience, skill, and knowledge, and statesmen of the proper caliber. As to the bankers, it might almost be said that the fact that there are many remaining in business, after the course of government during the last fourteen years, is proof of the existence of some who could qualify for their part of the task. There is, however, ample proof that many bankers saw trouble coming before 1929, followed wise policies, and did their best to persuade others, including the Government itself, to do so. It seems that there is sufficient talent of that kind for the purpose of administering the commercial and financial part of the Standard.

The outlook is darkest as to statesmanship, the task of which is to prepare and enact the proper laws, and to administer them correctly. Yet even here there is a ray of hope, and perhaps it is time to change from the pessimistic view to the optimistic, although that does involve ignoring all the monetary legislation of the last two years, as well as most of that of other kinds. In one respect it may be said to be an unfortunate accident that there has not already been taken the most important step toward the creation by the United States of an International Standard, and that is to make the dollar a monetary unit which may be freely acquired with the goods of other nations. Although not in exactly that language, the Democratic platform of 1932, which was overwhelmingly approved by the voters, gave such a promise. Furthermore, it declared in favor of a sound currency, to be maintained at all hazards. Had those promises been fulfilled, we should have been well advanced toward the establishment of a workable

Standard, instead of being in the position of having destroyed all remaining vestiges of such a Standard, and of calling upon the other nations to create one so that we may follow them in adopting it. Perhaps the people will learn before their present leaders do.

Although at present it may seem hopeless to discuss the removal of inflationary possibilities from our monetary laws, that is a necessary step. It is remarkable that, with all the criticism there has been of the Banking Act of 1935, there has been no attention directed to the fact that the gold-reserve principle of two and one half to one, contained in the Federal Reserve Act, is continued. That was a cause of much of our present difficulty, and that provision is the really objectionable feature of the recent Act. A distinction which must be learned in the United States is that between a commercial contract to deliver gold and a contract made by a government to deliver gold. Indeed, the metalistic conception of money is one which should be removed completely from our laws. To say that gold is necessary for use as a part of the Standard for commerce among nations is not to say that it is a thing out of which money may be manufactured. In this respect, it may be advisable to go further than any nation ever has gone, and to provide that gold shall not be used to create any money, but shall be treated as a commodity for sale at a fixed price by the head of the banking system. It is also important to get the gold out of the Treasury, and return it to its proper commercial use.

If its power to create money is wisely used, the United States requires not one dollar's worth of gold to create all the money needed for its internal circulation. Even if all the gold should be sent from the country, the Government could impose upon a properly organized Central Bank the obligation to sell gold at the old price of 23.22 grains per dollar, and, provided there were no dollars issued in addition to those now outstanding, that obligation could be discharged with the greatest ease just as soon as the Bank could have time to bring some gold in from abroad.

The use of several different kinds of notes should be abandoned, and the currency structure simplified by having one kind of note only. That should be one issued by the Government, with a denial of the note-issuing privilege to any part of the banking system. At present, there is the best kind of opportunity to do this on sound principles so that there would be no disturbance whatsoever. The first step would be one of several changes in the existing system of banks, by establishing a real Central Bank as the successor of the Federal Reserve Banks. Gold certificates issued by the Government are held by all the Federal Reserve Banks in excess of five thousand million dollars. The gold should be delivered to the Central Bank, in exchange for the certificates acquired from its predecessors, the Reserve Banks. Then the Treasury could be authorized to issue Government notes in the amount necessary to retire all Federal Reserve notes, and required to buy with such notes all Government bonds received by the new Central Bank from the Federal Reserve Banks. The amount of the new notes remaining after that purchase would be approximately enough to retire all silver certificates. A small amount of additional notes would be necessary to retire Federal Reserve Bank notes and silver dollars. As national bank notes are now being retired, that would leave only one kind of note. The present Government notes would be retained, but changed in form, and the subsidiary coinage would be retained as it is. This provides for replacing the money in circulation, other than subsidiary coins, and would put the Note Issue at approximately five thousand millions. Perhaps an additional five hundred millions would be required as emergency currency to be held by the Treasury.

Each of these notes would carry the guaranty of the United States that the Central Bank would sell gold for them at the rate of thirty-five dollars per ounce when tendered in amounts not less than a certain minimum. They would also bear a statement of their denomination and the fact that they were receivable as such in all payments due the United States. As the Central Bank would begin business with about five thousand million dollars' worth of gold, there would be no doubt of its ability to sell gold as required by commerce with other nations, or for internal use. With respect to gold, the purchasing power of an issue of money in this amount would be ample. In fact, the price of thirty-five dollars per ounce would be too high; and it should be reduced to the old price of twenty dollars and sixty-seven cents.

The amount of money created in this manner, including subsidiary coins, would be approximately six thousand millions. That amount should remain fixed, until an increase in national wealth called for additional money — according to the method of estimating that, set forth in the preceding chapter. The authority to calculate and provide for that slight increase should be delegated by Congress but remain subject to its control.

Although on first impression it may seem that the suggestion is to limit the amount of money unduly, it is to be remembered that in the days of prosperity, when more business was being done, the money in circulation was nearly one thousand million dollars less than it is now. The contracts of the banks to pay money were also then far greater than they are now, and that by several thousand millions. Furthermore, with a properly organized system of banks, to which subject attention must now be given, the requirements for money would be much less.

The duties of the Central Bank would be to buy and sell gold, to keep the reserve accounts of the other banks, and to perform proper fiscal operations for the Government. Its charter would require it to buy gold at a fixed price, either by paying for it in money, or giving some one of the member banks a credit for it on its books. Sales of gold, also at a fixed price specified in the charter, would be either for money or by charging the account of one of the member banks. The Central Bank should have the privilege of selling gold at less than the fixed price, and also of buying it at a higher price, in order to meet emergencies.

As the Central Bank would not have the note-issuing privilege, which is the only reason for making one subject to the control of a government, it should be owned and controlled by its stockholding member banks. Perhaps it would be advisable to give the Government minority representation on its Board of Directors, but no more. Also, the Central Bank should be forbidden to lend great sums to the Government, and prohibited from buying United States bonds issued after the date of its establishment in excess of a reasonable amount. No reserve requirements should be specified as to either gold or money, but both should be left to sound management.

It is to be emphasized again that the duty of the National Government is to provide a system of banks whose ability to perform their contracts to pay money on demand will be unquestioned. With that done, other parts of the banking business may be left to the states. The dividing line, which is at least suggested, if not actually drawn, by the Constitution, is that the National Government should establish and regulate banks which make contracts to pay money on demand, and that the states should attend to those which make contracts to pay money at a fixed time. This division of control over the banking business, customarily regarded as consisting of the handling of demand deposits and time deposits, not only is analytically correct, but fits in with the necessity for a dual system of some kind in recognition of the Federal nature of our Government. The latter feature may, by some, be regarded as an undesirable one for retention in our Constitution; but it is there, and cannot be removed except by most improbable constitutional amendments. Also, it would be unwise to remove banking entirely from local control and influence. Small communities deserve adequate banking facilities; and there seems to be a determined opposition to complete denial of independence to the institutions which render such services. Complete reform, for the purpose of establishing a banking system which would be in accord with the Constitution and with the business and political customs of the people, would necessarily encounter many practical difficulties and cause some disturbance. The following suggestions are made with an attempt to take all these factors into consideration; nevertheless, they may contain some features which would be

expensive, although neither that nor any inconvenience would be permanent.

There should be established a National Bank for
each state, to be the only one in its state permitted
to make any kind of contract to pay money on demand. That would give it a state-wide monopoly of
the demand-deposit business, with its branches to be
established wherever required by public convenience
and necessity. The Secretary of the Treasury, or the
Comptroller of the Currency, might be given authority to require it to establish, or abandon, branches on
the petition of the state banking authorities. These
National Banks would not be allowed either to accept
time deposits or to lend money to anyone except to
other banks, chartered by the state in which located,
and stockholders in the National Bank. The entire
business of these National Banks would consist of
carrying all checking accounts, including the reserve
accounts of their stockholder banks, and lending
money to the latter.

The banks chartered by the states would handle all
savings accounts, make all loans to members of the
public, act as trustees and fiduciaries of other kinds,
as at present, and generally do all banking business
except receiving demand deposits. Such state banks

as become stockholders would be permitted to rediscount, or borrow, at the National Bank.

The amount of capital and the requirements for state banks as members would have to be determined for the National Bank according to local conditions in each state. No persons other than member banks would be permitted to become stockholders in the National Bank, which would be owned and controlled by those stockholders, subject to indirect regulation by the National Government and such agencies as it might establish for the purpose. The provisions of the charters of such National Banks may be easily supplied in detail.

All the forty-eight National Banks would be the stockholders of the Central Bank, with which they would keep their reserves. That Bank should be able so to conduct its affairs that emergency currency would not be needed, but if it were the Treasury would have some with which to meet the demands. In fact, there would be too much money; and in some respects such a change would resemble that made when the Federal Reserve System relieved the banks of the necessity of maintaining large cash reserves. There would be, however, this difference:

332

the amount of money would be greatly decreased, whereas the Federal Reserve Act increased it.

With a monetary organization of this kind, the people of the United States might learn that a great hoard of gold is more of an indication of poverty than of prosperity, and finally be persuaded to give to the world an International Standard of Trade, based on the dollar as a unit of money which will always buy gold and may always be bought with goods.

SECTION I

THE BANK OF ENGLAND

1694. Anno quinto & sexto Gulielmi & Mariae.

CAP. XX

An act for granting to their Majesties several rates and duties upon tunnage of ships and vessels, and upon beer, ale, and other liquors, for securing certain recompences and advantages in the said act mentioned, to such persons as shall voluntarily advance the sum of fifteen hundred thousand pounds, towards the carrying on the war against France.

Most gracious sovereigns,

We your majesties most dutiful and loyal subjects, the commons assembled in parliament, for the further supply of your Majesties extraordinary occasions, for and towards the necessary defence of your realms, do humbly present your Majesties with the further gift of the impositions, rates, and duties herein after mentioned; and do beseech your Majesties that it may be enacted: . . .

XIX. And be it further enacted by the authority aforesaid, That it shall and may be lawful to and for their Majesties, by commission under the great seal of *England,* to authorize and appoint any number of persons to take and receive all such voluntary subscriptions as shall be made on or before the first day of August, which shall be in the year of our Lord one thousand six hundred ninety four, by any person or persons, natives or foreigners, bodies politick or corporate, for and towards the raising and paying into the receipt of *Exchequer* the said sum of twelve hundred thousand pounds, part of the sum of fifteen hundred thousand pounds, and that the yearly sum of one hundred thousand pounds, part of the said yearly sum of one hundred and forty thousand pounds, arising by and out of the said duties and impositions before mentioned, shall be applied, issued, and directed, and is hereby appropriated, to the use and advantage of such person and persons, bodies politick and corporate, as shall make such voluntary subscriptions and payments, their heirs, successors, or assigns in the proportion hereafter mentioned (that is to say) that each weekly or other payment arising by and out of the duties and impositions granted by this act, shall, by the

336

auditor of the receipt of *Exchequer,* from time to time, as the same shall be paid in, be separated and divided into five seventh parts and two seventh parts, which is according to the proportion of the said yearly sum of one hundred thousand pounds, to the said yearly sum of one hundred and forty thousand pounds, which five seventh parts, of the said several payments arising by and out of the duties and impositions granted by this act, and so set apart, is and are hereby intended and appropriated for and towards the payment and satisfaction of the said yearly sum of one hundred thousand pounds, and shall from time to time be issued and paid, as the same shall come into the said receipt of *Exchequer,* to the uses and advantages of such subscribers and contributors, their heirs, successors, or assigns, as shall subscribe and contribute for and towards the raising and paying into the receipt of *Exchequer* the said sum of twelve hundred thousand pounds, part of the said sum of fifteen hundred thousand pounds.

XX. And be it further enacted, That it shall and may be lawful to and for their Majesties, by letters patents under the great seal of *England,* to limit, direct, and appoint, how and in what manner and proportions, and under what rules and directions, the said sum of twelve hundred thousand pounds, part of the said sum of fifteen hundred thousand pounds, and the said yearly sum of one hundred thousand pounds, part of the said yearly sum of one hundred and forty thousand pounds, and every or any part or proportion thereof, may be assignable or transferrable, assigned or transferred, to such person or persons only, as shall freely and voluntarily accept of the same, and not otherwise; and to incorporate all and every such subscribers and contributors, their heirs, successors, or assigns, to be one body corporate, and politick, by the name of *the governor and company of the bank of* England, and, by the same name of *the governor and company of the bank of* England, to have perpetual succession, and a common seal, and that they and their successors, by the name aforesaid, shall be able and capable in law to have, purchase, receive, possess, enjoy, and retain to them and their successors, lands, rents, tenements, and hereditaments, of what kind, nature, or quality soever; and also to sell, grant, demise, aliene, or dispose of the same, and by the same name to sue and implead, and be sued and impleaded, answer and be answered, in courts of record, or any other place whatsoever, and to do and execute all and singular other matters and things by the name aforesaid, that to them shall or may appertain to do; subject nevertheless to the proviso and condition of redemption hereinafter mentioned.

XXVI. And it is hereby enacted by the authority aforesaid, that the said corporation so to be made, shall not borrow or give security by bill, bond, covenant or agreement under their common seal for any more, further or other sum or sums of money, exceeding in the whole the sum of twelve hundred thousand pounds, so that they shall not owe at any one time more than the said sum, unless it be by act of parliament upon funds agreed in parliament; and in such case only such further sums as shall be so directed and allowed to be borrowed by parliament, and for such time only, until they shall be repaid such further sums as they shall borrow by such authority: and if any more, or further or other sum or sums of money shall be borrowed, taken up, lent, or advanced, under their common seal, or for payment of which any bond, bill, covenant or agreement, or other writing shall be made, sealed or given, under the common seal of the said corporation so to be made; then and in such case all and every person and persons who shall be a member or members of the said corporation, his and their respective heirs, executors, and administrators, shall in his and their respective private and personal capacities be chargeable with, and liable in proportion to their several shares or subscriptions to the repayment of such monies which shall be so borrowed, taken up or lent, with interest for the same, in such manner as if such security had been a security for payment of so much money, and interest for the same, sealed by such respective member or members of the said corporation, and delivered by him or them as their respective acts and deeds, in proportion to their several shares or subscriptions as aforesaid; and that in every such case an action of debt shall and may be brought, commenced, prosecuted and maintained in any of their Majesties courts of record at *Westminster,* by the respective creditor or creditors, to whom any such security under the common seal of the said corporation shall be made, or his or their respective executors or administrators, against all and every, or any one or more of the persons who shall be members of the said corporation, or any of their respective heirs, executors or administrators, in proportion to their respective shares or subscriptions as aforesaid, and therein recover and have judgment for him or them, in such and the like manner, as if such security were respectively sealed by the respective person or persons who shall be so sued, or his or their respective ancestor, or testator, or intestate, and by him and them executed and delivered, as his or their respective acts and deeds; any condition, covenant, or agreement, to be made to the contrary thereof in any wise notwithstanding: and if any condition, covenant, or agreement shall be made to the contrary, the same shall be, and is hereby declared to be void; any thing herein contained, or any law or usage to the contrary notwithstanding; and in such action or actions so to be brought, no privilege, protection, essoin, or wager of law, nor any more than one imparlance shall be allowed.

XXVII. And to the intent that their Majesties subjects may not be oppressed by the said corporation, by their monopolizing or ingrossing any sort of goods, wares or merchandizes, be it further declared and enacted by the authority aforesaid, That the said corporation to be made and created by this act, shall not at any time, during the continuance thereof, deal or trade, or permit or suffer any person or persons whatsoever either in trust or for the benefit of the same, to deal or trade with any of the stock, monies or effects of or any ways belonging to the said corporation, in the buying or selling of any goods, wares, or merchandizes whatsoever; and every person or persons, who shall so deal or trade, or by whose order or directions such dealing or trading shall be made, prosecuted, or managed, shall forfeit for every such dealing or trading, and every such order and directions, treble the value of the goods and merchandize so traded for, to such person or persons who shall sue for the same by action of debt, bill, plaint, or information, in any of their Majesties courts of record at *Westminster,* wherein no essoin, protection, nor other privilege whatsoever, nor any injunction, order or restraint, nor wager of law shall be allowed, nor any more than one imparlance.

XXVIII. Provided, That nothing herein contained shall any ways be construed to hinder the said corporation from dealing in bills of exchange, or in buying or selling bullion, gold, or silver, or in selling any goods, wares, or merchandize whatsoever, which shall really and *bona fide* be left or deposited with the said corporation for money lent and advanced thereon, and which shall not be redeemed at the time agreed on, or within three months after, or from selling such goods as shall or may be the produce of lands purchased by the said corporation.

XXIX. Provided always, and be it enacted by the authority aforesaid, That all and every bill or bills obligatory and of credit under the seal of the said corporation made or given to any person or persons, shall and may, by indorsement thereon under the hand of such person or persons, be assignable and assigned to any person or persons who shall voluntarily accept the same, and so by such assignee, *toties quoties,* by indorsement thereupon; and that such assignment and assignments, so to be made, shall absolutely vest and transfer the right and property in and unto such bill or bills obligatory and of credit, and the monies due upon the same; and that the assignee or assignees shall and may sue for, and maintain an action thereupon in his own name.

XXX. Provided always, and it is hereby further enacted, That if the governor, deputy governor, the directors, managers, assistants, or other members of the said corporation so to be established, shall upon the account of the said corporation, at any time

or times purchase any lands or revenues belonging
to the crown, or advance or lend to their Majesties,
their heirs or successors, any sum or sums of money,
by way of loan or anticipation, on any part or parts,
branch or branches, fund or funds of the revenues
now granted or belonging, or hereafter to be granted
or belonging to their Majesties, their heirs or successors, other than such fund or funds, part or parts,
branch or branches of the said revenues only, on
which a credit of loan is or shall be granted by
parliament; that then the said governor, deputy governor, directors, managers, or assistants, or other
members of the said corporation, who shall consent,
agree to, or approve of, the advancing or lending
to their Majesties, their heirs or successors, such
sum or sums of money as aforesaid, and each and
every of them so agreeing, consenting, or approving,
and being thereof lawfully convicted, shall for every
such offence forfeit treble the value of every such
sum or sums of money so lent, whereof one fifth
part shall be to the informer, to be recovered in any
of their Majesties courts of record at *Westminster,*
by action of debt, bill, plaint, or information, wherein
no protection, wager of law, essoin, privilege of
parliament, or other privilege shall be allowed, nor

344

any more than one imparlance; and the residue to be disposed of towards publick uses, as shall be directed by parliament, and not otherwise.

Note on the Charter of the Bank of England

The Charter of the Bank of England is set out in "The Statutory Rules & Orders Revised to Dec. 31, 1903" (generally abbreviated S.R. & O. Rev. 1904), Vol. I, subtitle "Bank of England," pp. 1–24. It is no more than a formal document in the nature of letters patent issued pursuant to the Act of Parliament, and relates, almost exclusively, to the details of organizing the Bank and certain of its bylaws.

The Act of the Congress of the United States establishing the first Bank of the United States was in itself a charter.

THE FIRST BANK OF THE
UNITED STATES

An act to incorporate the subscribers to the Bank of
the United States.

Feb. 25, 1791.

Whereas it is conceived that the establishment of
a bank for the United States, upon a foundation
sufficiently extensive to answer the purposes intended
thereby, and at the same time upon the principles
which afford adequate security for an upright and
prudent administration thereof, will be very condu-
cive to the successful conducting of the national finances; will tend to give facility to the obtaining of
loans, for the use of the government, in sudden
emergencies; and will be productive of considerable
advantages to trade and industry in general: Therefore,

Section 1. *Be it enacted by the Senate and House
of Representatives of the United States of America*

346

in Congress assembled, That a bank of the United States shall be established; the capital stock whereof shall not exceed ten millions of dollars, divided into twenty-five thousand shares, each share being four hundred dollars; and that subscriptions, towards constituting the said stock, shall, on the first Monday of April next, be opened at the city of Philadelphia, under the superintendence of such persons, not less than three, as shall be appointed for that purpose by the President of the United States (who is hereby empowered to appoint the said persons accordingly); which subscriptions shall continue open, until the whole of the said stock shall have been subscribed.

Sec. 2. *And be it further enacted,* That it shall be lawful for any person, co-partnership, or body politic, to subscribe for such or so many shares, as he, she, or they shall think fit, not exceeding one thousand, except as shall be hereafter directed relatively to the United States; and that the sums, respectively subscribed, except on behalf of the United States, shall be payable one fourth in gold and silver, and three fourths in that part of the public debt, which, according to the loan proposed in the fourth and fifteenth sections of the act, entitled "An act making provision for the debt of the United States," shall bear an accruing interest, at the time of payment, of six per centum per annum, and shall also be payable in four equal parts, in the aforesaid ratio of specie to debt, at the distance of six calendar months from each other; the first whereof shall be paid at the time of subscription.

Sec. 3. *And be it further enacted,* That all those, who shall become subscribers to the said bank, their successors and assigns, shall be, and are hereby created and made a corporation and body politic, by the name and style of *The President, Directors and Company, of the Bank of the United States;* and shall so continue, until the fourth day of March, one thousand eight hundred and eleven: And by that name, shall be, and are hereby made able and capable in law, to have, purchase, receive, possess, enjoy, and retain to them and their successors, lands, rents, tenements, hereditaments, goods, chattels and effects of what kind, nature or quality soever, to an amount, not exceeding in the whole fifteen millions of dollars, including the amount of the capital stock aforesaid; and the same to sell, grant, demise, aliene or dispose of; to sue and be sued, plead and be impleaded, answer and be answered, defend and be defended, in courts of record, or any other place whatsoever:

348

And also to make, have, and use a common seal, and the same to break, alter and renew, at their pleasure; and also to ordain, establish, and put in execution, such bylaws, ordinances and regulations, as shall seem necessary and convenient for the government of the said corporation, not being contrary to law, or to the constitution thereof (for which purpose, general meetings of the stockholders shall and may be called by the directors, and in the manner herein after specified), and generally to do and execute all and singular acts, matters and things, which to them it shall or may appertain to do; subject nevertheless to the rules, regulations, restrictions, limitations and provisions herein after prescribed and declared.

Sec. 4. *And be it further enacted,* That, for the well ordering of the affairs of the said corporation, there shall be twenty-five directors; of whom there shall be an election on the first Monday of January in each year, by the stockholders or proprietors of the capital stock of the said corporation, and by plurality of the votes actually given; and those who shall be duly chosen at any election, shall be capable of serving as directors, by virtue of such choice, until the end or expiration of the Monday of January next ensuing the time of such election, and no longer. And the said directors, at their first meeting after each election, shall choose one of their number as President.

Sec. 5. *Provided always, and be it further enacted,* That, as soon as the sum of four hundred thousand dollars, in gold and silver, shall have been actually received on account of the subscriptions to the said stock, notice thereof shall be given, by the persons under whose superintendence the same shall have been made, in at least two public gazettes printed in the city of Philadelphia; and the said persons shall, at the same time in like manner, notify a time and place within the said city, at the distance of ninety days from the time of such notification, for proceeding to the election of directors; and it shall be lawful for such election to be then and there made; and the persons, who shall then and there be chosen, shall be the first directors, and shall be capable of serving, by virtue of such choice, until the end or expiration of the Monday in January next ensuing the time of making the same, and shall forthwith thereafter commence the operations of the said bank, at the said city of Philadelphia. *And provided further,* That, in case it should at any time happen, that an election of directors should not be made upon any day when pursuant to this act it ought to have been made, the said corporation shall not, for that cause, be deemed to be dissolved; but it shall be lawful, on any other day, to hold and make an election of directors in such manner as shall have been regulated by the laws and ordinances of the said corporation. *And provided lastly,* That, in case of the death, resignation, absence from the United States, or removal of a director by the stockholders, his place may be filled up, by a new choice, for the remainder of the year.

Sec. 6. *And be it further enacted,* That the directors for the time being shall have power to appoint such officers, clerks, and servants under them, as shall be necessary for executing the business of the said corporation, and to allow them such compensation, for their services respectively, as shall be reasonable; and shall be capable of exercising such other powers and authorities, for the well governing and ordering of the affairs of the said corporation, as shall be described, fixed, and determined by the laws, regulations, and ordinances of the same.

Sec. 7. *And be it further enacted,* That the following rules, restrictions, limitations and provisions, shall form and be fundamental articles of the constitution of the said corporation, viz.

I. The number of votes to which each stockholder shall be entitled, shall be according to the number of shares he shall hold, in the proportions following: That is to say, for one share, and not more than two shares, one vote: for every two shares above two, and not exceeding ten, one vote: for every four shares above ten, and not exceeding thirty, one vote: for every six shares above thirty, and not exceeding sixty, one vote: for every eight shares above sixty, and not exceeding one hundred, one vote: and for every ten shares above one hundred, one vote: — But no person, co-partnership, or body politic shall be entitled to a greater number than thirty votes. And after the first election, no share or shares shall confer a right of suffrage, which shall not have been holden three calendar months previous to the day of election. Stockholders actually resident within the United States, and none other, may vote in elections by proxy.

II. Not more than three fourths of the directors in office, exclusive of the president, shall be eligible for the next succeeding year: but the director, who shall be president at the time of an election, may always be re-elected.

III. None but a stockholder, being a citizen of the United States, shall be eligible as a director.

IV. No director shall be entitled to any emolument, unless the same shall have been allowed by the stockholders at a general meeting. The stockholders shall make such compensation to the president, for his extraordinary attendance at the bank, as shall appear to them reasonable.

V. Not less than seven directors shall constitute a board for the transaction of business, of whom, the president shall always be one, except in case of sickness, or necessary absence; in which case his place may be supplied by any other director, whom he, by writing under his hand, shall nominate for the purpose.

VI. Any number of stockholders, not less than sixty, who, together, shall be proprietors of two hundred shares or upwards, shall have power at any time to call a general meeting of the stockholders, for purposes relative to the institution, giving at least ten weeks' notice, in two public gazettes of the place where the bank is kept, and specifying, in such notice, the object or objects of such meeting.

VII. Every cashier or treasurer, before he enters upon the duties of his office, shall be required to give bond, with two or more sureties, to the satisfaction of the directors, in a sum not less than fifty thousand dollars, with condition for his good behaviour.

VIII. The lands, tenements and hereditaments which it shall be lawful for the said corporation to hold, shall be only such as shall be requisite for its immediate accommodation in relation to the convenient transacting of its business, and such as shall have been *bona fide* mortgaged to it by way of security, or conveyed to it in satisfaction of debts previously contracted in the course of its dealings, or purchased at sales upon judgments which shall have been obtained for such debts.

IX. The total amount of the debts, which the said corporation shall at any time owe, whether by bond, bill, note, or other contract, shall not exceed the sum of ten millions of dollars, over and above the monies then actually deposited in the bank for safe keeping, unless the contracting of any greater debt shall have been previously authorized by a law of the United States. In case of excess, the directors, under whose administration it shall happen, shall be liable for the same, in their natural and private capacities; and an action of debt may, in such case, be brought against them, or any of them, their or any of their heirs, executors or administrators, in any court of record of the United States, or of either of them, by any creditor or creditors of the said corporation, and may be prosecuted to judgment and execution; any condition, covenant, or agreement to the contrary notwithstanding. But this shall not be construed to exempt the said corporation, or the lands, tenements, goods or chattels of the same, from being also liable for and chargeable with the said excess. Such of the said directors, who may have been absent when the said excess was contracted or created, or who may have dissented from the resolution or act whereby the same was so contracted or created, may respectively exonerate themselves from being so liable, by forthwith giving notice of the fact, and of their absence or dissent, to the President of the United States, and to the stockholders, at a general meeting, which they shall have power to call for that purpose.

X. The said corporation may sell any part of the public debt whereof its stock shall be composed, but shall not be at liberty to purchase any public debt whatsoever; nor shall directly or indirectly deal or trade in any thing, except bills of exchange, gold or silver bullion, or in the sale of goods really and truly pledged for money lent and not redeemed in due time; or of goods which shall be the produce of its lands. Neither shall the said corporation take more than at the rate of six per centum per annum, for or upon its loans or discounts.

XI. No loan shall be made by the said corporation, for the use or on account of the government of the United States, to an amount exceeding one hundred thousand dollars, or of any particular state, to an amount exceeding fifty thousand dollars, or of any foreign prince or state, unless previously authorized by a law of the United States.

XII. The stock of the said corporation shall be assignable and transferable, according to such rules as shall be instituted in that behalf, by the laws and ordinances of the same.

XIII. The bills obligatory and of credit, under the seal of the said corporation, which shall be made to any person or persons, shall be assignable by indorsement thereupon, under the hand or hands of such person or persons, and of his, her, or their assignee or assignees, and so as absolutely to transfer and vest the property thereof in each and every assignee or assignees successively, and to enable such assignee or assignees to bring and maintain an action thereupon in his, her, or their own name or names. And bills or notes, which may be issued by order of the said corporation, signed by the president, and countersigned by the principal cashier or treasurer thereof, promising the payment of money to any person or persons, his, her, or their order, or to bearer, though not under the seal of the said corporation, shall be binding and obligatory upon the same, in the like manner, and with the like force and effect, as upon any private person or persons, if issued by him or them, in his, her, or their private or natural capacity or capacities; and shall be assignable and negotiable, in like manner, as if they were so issued by such private person or persons — that is to say, those which shall be payable to any person or persons, his, her, or their order, shall be assignable by indorsement, in like manner, and with the like effect, as foreign bills of exchange now are; and those which are payable to bearer, shall be negotiable and assignable by delivery only.

XIV. Half yearly dividends shall be made of so much of the profits of the bank, as shall appear to the directors advisable; and once in every three years, the directors shall lay before the stockholders, at a general meeting, for their information, an exact and particular statement of the debts, which shall have remained unpaid after the expiration of the original credit, for a period of treble the term of that credit; and of the surplus of profit, if any, after deducting losses and dividends. If there shall be a failure in the payment of any part of any sum, subscribed by any person, co-partnership, or body politic, the party failing shall lose the benefit of any dividend, which may have accrued, prior to the time for making such payment, and during the delay of the same.

XV. It shall be lawful for the directors aforesaid, to establish offices wheresoever they shall think fit, within the United States, for the purposes of discount and deposit only, and upon the same terms, and in the same manner, as shall be practised at the bank; and to commit the management of the said offices, and the making of the said discounts, to such persons, under such agreements, and subject to such regulations as they shall deem proper; not being contrary to law, or to the constitution of the bank.

XVI. The officer at the head of the treasury department of the United States, shall be furnished, from time to time, as often as he may require, not exceeding once a week, with statements of the amount of the capital stock of the said corporation, and of the debts due to the same; of the monies deposited therein; of the notes in circulation, and of the cash in hand; and shall have a right to inspect such general accounts in the books of the bank, as shall relate to the said statements. *Provided,* That this shall not be construed to imply a right of inspecting the account of any private individual or individuals with the bank.

Sec. 8. *And be it further enacted,* That if the said corporation, or any person or persons for or to the use of the same, shall deal or trade in buying or selling any goods, wares, merchandise, or commodities whatsoever, contrary to the provisions of this act, all and every person and persons, by whom any order or direction for so dealing or trading shall have been given, and all and every person and persons who shall have been concerned as parties or agents therein, shall forfeit and lose treble the value of the goods, wares, merchandises, and commodities, in which such dealing and trade shall have been; one half thereof to the use of the informer, and the other half thereof to the use of the United States, to be recovered with costs of suit.

Sec. 9. *And be it further enacted,* That if the said corporation shall advance or lend any sum, for the use or on account of the government of the United States, to an amount exceeding one hundred thousand dollars; or of any particular state to an amount exceeding fifty thousand dollars; or of any foreign prince or state, (unless previously authorized thereto by a law of the United States,) all and every person and persons, by and with whose order, agreement, consent, approbation, or connivance, such unlawful advance or loan shall have been made, upon conviction thereof, shall forfeit and pay, for every such offence, treble the value or amount of the sum or sums which shall have been so unlawfully advanced or lent; one fifth thereof to the use of the informer, and the residue thereof to the use of the United States; to be disposed of by law and not otherwise.

Sec. 10. *And be it further enacted,* That the bills or notes of the said corporation, originally made payable, or which shall have become payable on demand, in gold and silver coin, shall be receivable in all payments to the United States.

Sec. 11. *And be it further enacted,* That it shall be lawful for the President of the United States, at any time or times, within eighteen months after the first day of April next, to cause a subscription to be made to the stock of the said corporation, as part of the aforesaid capital stock of ten millions of dollars, on behalf of the United States, to an amount not exceeding two millions of dollars; to be paid out of the monies which shall be borrowed by virtue of either of the acts, the one entitled "An act making provision for the debt of the United States;" and the other entitled "An act making provision for the reduction of the public debt;" borrowing of the bank an equal sum, to be applied to the purposes, for which the said monies shall have been procured; reimbursable in ten years, by equal annual instalments; or at any time sooner, or in any greater proportions, that the government may think fit.

Sec. 12. *And be it further enacted,* That no other bank shall be established by any future law of the United States, during the continuance of the corporation hereby created; for which the faith of the United States is hereby pledged.

Approved, February 25, 1791.

INDEX

363

INDEX

silver, 71; at premium for taxes, 72; lower value of, 76–7; fixed price of, 77; and Act of 1816, 116

HAMILTON, ALEXANDER, tax-coinage problem recognized, 29; quoted on money and taxes, 43–4; and Great Britain, 46, 61; first Secretary of Treasury, 93; and national debt, 93–5; outlines tax program, 94–6; and national bank, 95–6; and Bank of U. S., 97; and limitation on note issues, 99; and Fiduciary Issue of notes, 101–2; and world's masterpiece of legal argument, 102; and Jefferson, 102–3, 105; criticism of, 103–4; and the Mint, 105; and Mint ratio, 107; and bimetalism, 107; and silver overvaluation reason, 108; and circulation of small coins, 109; and prosperity, 109–10; high praise of, 110; System abandoned, 145–57; and state bank notes, 149–50; and charter of second Bank of U. S., 150–1; and Mint Act of 1792, 181; and Elihu Root, 210; quoted on power to tax, 261

INCOME, governmental, 51; individual, 51
Industrial Revolution, effect of, 52

JACKSON, PRESIDENT, and Jacksonian System, 157–170; and state bank notes, 157, 159–60; and Biddle, 158; and

Bank of U. S., 157–61; and Panic of 1837, 161; and Specie Circular, 163; defects of System, 167–8; System and farmers, 168–9; System and Hamilton System, 169; System abandoned, 170
Jefferson, and Hamilton, 102–3; and decimal system, 105–6; and silver standard, 107

LAW MERCHANT, strength of, 36; and *pie poudre,* 36; and Lord Mansfield, 37 and *n.*
Legal tender, defined, 41; law of in England, 66; and notes of Continental Congress, 90; and notes of States, 90; and Bank Charter Act of 1833, 121; and Congress, 174–5; Cases and Gold Clause Cases, 280–1

MERCHANTS, and bills of exchange, 83; as bankers, 84
Metals, *see* Precious Metals
Monetary process, 11; principles of, 11–13; breakdown of, 36; revival of, 36–7; scope of, 45; in England, 61; and Alexander Hamilton, 61, 87, 93; of Colonies, 88; principles and Great Britain, 134–5
Monetary use of gold, prejudice against, 17; fallacies regarding, 17
Money, an instrument of distribution, 3–5; "Great Wheel of Circulation," 4; developed by status method of distribution, 10, 14; common denominator for terms of contract, 10; and Law